But I Digress ...

Daily Profiles and Punditry
from the Sacramento Business Journal

Ed Goldman

Published by the
Sacramento Business Journal
1400 X St.
Sacramento, CA 95818

ISBN 978-1484894453
Printed in the United States of America
First printing — May 2013

Editor: Jack Robinson
Cover design by Jeff Byrd

To order copies of this book, contact the
Sacramento Business Journal at 916-447-7661

Contents

FUNNY BUSINESS

CELEBRITIES I HAVE PRETENDED TO KNOW

TOIL, TROUBLE & TRAVEL

ENTREPRENEURS AND OTHER SUPERHEROES

WHAT ARE THEY THINKING?

CORPORATE EXECS

TECHNOLOGY

OFFICIALS, LAWYERS AND POLITICOS (OH, MY!)

HUMAN FRAILTIES

AUTHORS, ARTISTS AND ENTERTAINERS

GOOD INTENTIONS

ARTS ORGANIZERS AND EDUCATORS

OF MEDIA AND MARKETING

COMMUNITY MEMBERS AND LEADERS

Foreword

The Sacramento Business Journal is all about the nuts and bolts of the local economy. You won't find a features section in this newspaper. No movie reviews or stories about this year's patio furniture. No comics — not even Dilbert.

So I sometimes I get asked: What's Ed Goldman doing in the paper?

Most often it's people in the news business who ask. It's telling that I don't hear the question from readers. I think they understand Ed's role as a daily blogger and weekly columnist in the print edition: He explores the texture, the culture and the people of our business community.

Ed has the credentials to do it. He's a marketing veteran who has worked for public agencies and private companies. He has run his own shop. He knows the capital business community, its leaders — and the history and relationships that shape it today. His early career as a journalist gives him the reporting and writing skills to tell stories. And his unstoppable sense of fun gives us all something to smile at — or groan about— every weekday morning.

I'm pleased to present this collection of Ed's columns. Readers who saw them online or in print will certainly find their favorites among them. And those who missed them the first time around will discover some gems of insight into our world.

Jack Robinson
Editor, Sacramento Business Journal

Author's note

In August of 2011, I began to write a five-times-weekly column for the Sacramento Business Journal. Friends and enemies, sometimes wearing identical clothes and going by the same surnames, warned that the rigors of producing wildly humorous, continually enlightening and occasionally moving columns with that frequency (around 260 a year, give or take a holiday) would prove maddening.

I completely agreed, which is why only a handful of my columns, at best, can be said to be wildly humorous, continually enlightening or occasionally moving. I'd also advise you to check the credentials of whoever said even a handful could be.

What I try to do each day is simply offer a slightly screwy or unpleasantly direct glimpse of business life here and elsewhere. On some days my column may not even seem to have much to do with business (such as when I write about being addicted to the Encore Westerns channel or about my irrational contempt for government-funded studies of sarcasm). And that's because on those days, they really don't.

I've tried to remain mostly apolitical in the column even though, in my allegedly real life, I'm a staunch believer in believing almost nothing that elected officials, and some appointed ones, tell me. This goes double for the airport security cop who nodded that it was fine for me to help someone get her bag to curbside check-in, then gave me a ticket for leaving my car unattended for perhaps three minutes, in full view of him. Couldn't he have even whispered in my general direction what his intentions were?

I also tend to mistrust — for the word "distrust" implies that at one time, I did trust — almost anyone who tells me, "I'm this kind of person," or words to that effect. My experience, after spending a bit more than 62 years with the

Department of Earth, is that people are rarely the "kind of" people they say they are. People are what they do and how they behave. Those tend to show what they believe. Even so, when they begin sentences with the phrase, "At the end of the day," they're to be tolerated but never to be invited to ocarina festivals.

This book covers everything from my encounters with Wikipedia founder Jimmy Wales and Dr. Mehmet Oz to my quixotic quest for the perfect local tuna sandwich. And while I'm certainly not in the league, nor believe the most famous comment, of Will Rogers, who said he'd never met a man he didn't like, I can tell you that all the people I've interviewed for this column are people I not only liked but probably still would if they'd return my calls, emails and texts.

Thanks for inviting me to your hard-earned spare time.

Ed Goldman
May 2013

Acknowledgements

If one is going to write columns intended to be humorous, it's beyond helpful to have an editor who realizes that even when they verge on the slapstick, tasteless or politically knuckle-headed, they're still closer to soufflés than scrambled eggs. Jack Robinson, the editor of the Sacramento Business Journal, has handled my work with the utmost care and professionalism. He's been encouraging and, when necessary, stern. I thank him many times over for his sharp eye and sense of fun.

Melissa Wiese, the Business Journal's social-media editor, who found always appropriate and often hilarious ways to illustrate my columns, has also been a wonderful co-conspirator, and if I wore a hat or drank sherry, I'd tip it or dip it in homage to her contributions.

I'd also like to thank all of our readers, even the ones who've suggested from time to time that it may be prudent for me to consider another line of work.

For Valerie V

FUNNY BUSINESS

Laughter is a good career move

Since founding my marketing/PR business in 1982, it has afforded me continual opportunities to delve into a variety of industries: water, construction, insurance, entertainment, government, finance, agriculture, economic development, medical, law, and engineering, among others.

When I tackle the needs of a field I don't initially know a good deal about, I feel like a method actor learning a part or, better yet, like Lt. Columbo familiarizing himself with his suspect's world by learning (some cherished episodes come to mind) all about wine or cinematic special effects, military strategy or shipping timetables.

Unfortunately, the only universal truth I've gleaned from all of this role-playing and investigating is this: To succeed in business, almost any business, you'd better develop a good, hearty laugh.

Think about most of the meetings you attend: gales of laughter, at least at the beginning and end. (Rotary and Kiwanis meetings don't count: for some reason, members start laughing there the minute they walk in the door and don't stop until they cackle their way back to their cars. There must be something in the chicken.)

As you know, you don't need to have an actual sense of humor to have a hearty laugh. When you think about it, very few of us are laugh riots. Life's just not that amusing, especially if you find yourself, unprepared, on its downward slope — physically, economically, spiritually, domestically. Yes, I'm talking about a crowded slope.

We all want to laugh, though, and that's the real joy of make-believe merriment. Sometimes, if I've been set up effectively (i.e., someone says I write amusing columns or plays), I can start a group chuckling by just saying something off-handedly non-brilliant like, "Now, where were we?" Or, if I get a flattering introduction as a speaker, by saying, "Thanks for those kind words. I'm glad you could read my handwriting."

Neither is a sidesplitting line. But in a social context, where almost none of us are all that comfortable to begin with, simple irreverence can win the day.

Laughter can be a generous, inexpensive gift, one that some people are capable of providing on a moment's notice. The downside is that this can sometimes encourage people who tell interminable stories — maybe even throwing in unrecognizable imitations of all of the characters' voices — that they're just one step away from taking over Jon Stewart's show on Comedy Central.

So work on your chortle and guffaw. Learn to wipe an imaginary tear from one eye because, dammit, this is just all too hilarious. And don't worry: You can drop this nonsense when you reach the top of your field. At that point, everyone will be laughing heartily at your every quip.

Home-office headaches

A Chicago writer, Chuck Green, wrote a nice piece for the Wall Street Journal this week about having one's office at home. In it, he referenced a 2007 Census Bureau report that indicated more than 50 percent of all businesses are operated out of the owner's home.

He also reported on one of the dangers of doing so: Your clients may not see your home office as anything but a home, and act accordingly by wandering over to the fridge to help themselves to a soda or, in one of the cases reported, going upstairs to your bedroom and grabbing a quick nap.

I've worked out of an office in my home full-time since 1984 and have never dealt with either of these somewhat comical mishaps. But once, when I won a substantial project from a state agency, the contracts officer asked if she and her management team could tour my agency before we signed the paperwork.

At the time, I lived in a two-bedroom, one-bath home in East Sacramento. It would be, I decided, a very brief tour. I considered including the backyard, which was narrow but quite long: an alleyway was originally supposed to run along the back of the property but the city either canceled its plans to build it or simply forgot about it — a classic example of what I often refer to as Your Government Inaction.

The tour request was a result of a natural misunderstanding. Because my company is incorporated, and because I'd brought some reliable subcontractors to the interview, the contracts officer figured that my company consisted of more than just your faithful correspondent. While I'd never indicated otherwise, I certainly hadn't done anything in the interview to disabuse anyone of the notion that Goldman Communications Inc. was a vast, globe-girdling media, public relations and advertising mega-agency. (Oh, I might have mentioned Paris, Helsinki and Prague in passing but only to suggest I liked their names.)

The tour never happened, mainly because it proved too difficult to coordinate four people's calendars; it was, as now, that ominous scheduling time of year called Close to the Holidays. Everyone had vacation, personal health or even planned sick days to take. This was also at the start of the state's "flex time" initiative, which made getting people together in one room at the same time as futile as falling in love with Kim Kardashian. She, by the way, has never requested a tour of my office.

Casualty Friday

As a quick glance at the person sitting in the next office or cubicle wearing flip-flops, cutoffs and a wife-beater T-shirt will attest, the other day was Casual Friday. For years I've referred to it as Casualty Friday: the one perk an employer can offer to employees that doesn't cost the employer a dime (unless the employer places a cash value on, say, dignity, decorum and clean toenails).

I realize that not every business or nonprofit is in a position to offer this extraordinary benefit. If your clients or customers actually visit your offices, chances are you don't want them to think they've mistakenly stumbled into a remake of Deliverance featuring the original costumes. I know that some companies still maintain some sort of dress code even on Casualty Friday (these are called smart companies). And I have to confess that when I sit in my home office and write this column, or confer by phone or cyberspace with my marketing clients, I'm not usually inclined to do so while wearing the nifty three-piece suit I bought from S. Benson & Company last year.

In truth, I don't wear that suit to too many interviews or meetings, either. I look less like a consultant in it than a mob enforcer named Vinnie the Lip. Maybe I shouldn't carry such a large iPhone in my breast pocket.

Quitting Time

The Wall Street Journal reported last week that "sappy goodbye emails" or nasty farewell blasts can have an unnerving effect at companies — and, I'm sure, at nonprofit organizations. I experienced the latter several years ago when a fundraiser, whom I fought with my theater company's volunteer board to hire, turned out to be a minor disappointment, in the same way that falling out of the Goodyear Blimp onto your head can be termed a minor disappointment. The person was provided the opportunity to resign rather than be fired or, as some members suggested, boiled in canola oil. The person quit, all right, but not before sending a blistering message to the entire board, including me, the person's admittedly misguided champion, telling us what idiots we all were.

The problems of sending universal bye-byes can be manifold.

If, for example, you happen to be on someone's email list simply by virtue of your not having moved fast enough to unsubscribe, label the sender a spammer or obtain a restraining order (my preferred method of deterrence), you might receive that highly maudlin missive or intensely homicidal adieu and react like this when noting who sent it: "Who is this?"

On the other hand, if you know the sender, you may be offended to find that he or she had a sentimental affection for everyone in the workplace — in short, not just for you, despite those incisive chats you enjoyed when passing each other each day in the hallway ("How ya doin'?" "OK, for a Tuesday!").

It may also unsettle you if the sender does a global vent in his or her valedictorian message ("You're all mediocre creeps and I'm glad I won't ever see you again, not even in Heaven or Home Depot"). "Geez," you may think, "I may be mediocre but when did I ever give the impression that I'm also a creep?" (Alternatively, "Geez, I may be a creep but why would you call me mediocre?" Final alternative: "I'm sorry, I don't happen to believe there's any such place as Home Depot.")

I think it's an interesting dilemma even though I've never resigned from a job, client, publication or marriage via email blast. I've been tempted, of course, to write a furious message and then send a "bcc" to my exclusive address book, which now numbers in the thousands thanks to all of those people who send email blasts and reveal the addresses — via the cc field — of everyone who's receiving it. Helpful cyber hint: This is why the concept of "bcc" was invented long ago, back when we sent memos on something called "paper" and dinosaurs roamed the earth.

My solution is simplicity myself (unfortunately, this is also my nickname in Mensa circles): If you're leaving a workplace, just leave. Those who miss you or those to whom you owe some money will seek you out. Just don't answer the door to anyone holding a bottle of canola oil.

Multi-disastering

To start off the week on the wrong foot, let's talk about multi-tasking. If you're simply too swamped, buried or fully committed to hang around until the end of this clog, here's its insta-moral: Most of the people who tell me they're multi-taskers aren't. They're multi-gaspers.

True multi-taskers have neither the time nor the inclination to characterize themselves as such. They rarely tell you how swamped, buried or fully committed they are because when they truly are, they're not going to waste potentially productive moments narrating their challenges.

Only people who are what I call meta-busy (it used to be called officious) feel it's important to stop what they're doing to discuss what you just stopped them from doing. They multi-gasp. "I can't talk right now," they say — often via email, Twitter or live. Then they'll take several more minutes to tell you why.

I think I speak for many of us when I ask: Who the hell cares?

And as that all-important follow-up question: What makes you think you're the only one who's busy?

This topic has a particular resonance for me. I've kept myself, and frequently those I love, in kibble for most of my adult life by doing exactly what my high school counselors told me I shouldn't do: spread myself too thin. When I was in my teens, I loved to draw, write, sing, compose music, paint and chase girls. While I never expected to be paid for the latter, I've somehow managed, for many years, to cobble together an income by combining or engaging separately in all of the above. I've never viewed it as multi-tasking. For me, I've always referred to it as making a living.

I think perhaps that multi-tasking is akin to eccentricity: the true practitioners of each have no idea they are.

I'd write more about this but I have to go back to spreading myself too thin. I wish it would extend to my waist size.

Staff infection

For someone who's been married three times and never forgot an anniversary, this is embarrassing. I forgot the 30th anniversary of my own business.

In fact, it took my friend Darlena Belushin McKay, managing editor of Sacramento Magazine, to point it out to me in a congratulatory note. She had noticed these words, following my name, at the bottom of an email I'd sent her: "Goldman Communications. Founded 1982." In short, she had done the math. I hadn't.

Actually, I'm not sure what I'd have done if I'd noticed. While I realize that most companies celebrate their anniversaries, I'm also cognizant of the fact that most companies are larger than mine. And most aren't operated out of a spare bedroom in the CEO's home. Allow me to clarify:

- The only way to lengthen my daily home-to-office commute would be if I were to move into a larger house.
- The only way for me to increase the size of my staff is by gaining weight.
- I'm always voted Employee of the Month and Best Boss ever.
- The annual office picnic consists of my taking a sandwich and soda into the backyard and staging a two-legged race.

Working for myself has its advantages, especially when the holiday season kicks in. I can throw an office party, drink too much, insult myself and get to bed early rather than hang around and spend the rest of the night apologizing to me.

I don't have to pretend to enjoy the rum balls made by Midge from Accounting. And I don't have to play Secret Santa for anyone but me. (I can't wait to see what I give myself this year.)

I know that a lot of you out there are either sole practitioners or have extremely small staffs. If you get a moment, I'd love to hear if you miss being in a heavily populated workplace — and if so, what on earth do you miss about it?

Oops. Time to get back to work. My boss is on my case. I can't wait to insult him at the office party.

Startling news about office flirting

S ince it never once occurred to you or me, I'm happy to report that a series of academic studies has concluded that some flirting in the workplace is fine but some of it (and this is crucial) really isn't. It's just as we suspected but were hesitant to say aloud for fear of being mocked.

The Wall Street Journal reported on some Northern Illinois University studies last week that discussed the motivations for flirting and what exactly constitutes it. If you weren't sure about it, placing your hand on a co-worker's arm might be OK, but not always; whereas (and I'm adding this in the interest of intellectual clarity) putting it on a co-worker's pants is generally considered imprudent.

I'm not telling you any of this not because I think you didn't know but because many of you have told me you share my highly skeptical view of government-funded studies that, after painstaking research and thousands upon thousands of dollars, reveal the patently obvious or remarkably uninteresting.

I've written about a few of these in this column. Studies have been done recently on detecting sarcasm in emails and tweets, how too much sitting is unhealthy for us, how some people perceive that men with shaved heads are more masculine, and the fact that skinny monkeys don't necessarily live longer than pudgy monkeys.

All of these studies produced important findings — if you happen to be someone whose friends are heavily into snarky messages, whose office chair is too comfortable to leave, who's losing his hair and who's also a pudgy monkey, respectively.

The professor who assembled the research said the motivations for flirting are having fun, boosting self-esteem, gauging interest, reinforcing a relationship and finding a mate. He left out killing time, trying to get a promotion and checking to see if the person you're flirting with has had an obvious facelift.

Maybe those will be covered in the next study.

The ideal business lunch

Some of my better business lunches are spent in busy restaurants. Alone.

While I rarely come away with a new client or a job offer, I characterize the experience as continuing education (and hope the IRS will agree). I learn anew that I'm neither terribly private nor painfully shy. I usually run into a person or two that I know and, by virtue of my photo appearing with this clog, a person or two, excluding the bartender, who know who I am. (I threw a wrench into this after my recent operation by growing back the beard I'd sported for many years. But since it came in gray and appears vaguely biblical, it'll probably come off after the holidays.)

For many people, including the late playwright Tennessee Williams, eating alone in a public place creates an almost morbid discomfort. And I realize that if you don't have anyone in your life, eating alone can underline your loneliness; it certainly has for me during the partner-less times in my adult life. But if you bring something to read or work on, provided it's not a plumbing repair job, it's amazing how peaceful it can be when people all around you are talking and laughing — and you're not required to join in.

A CEO I know, now retired, used to take himself to lunch at least three days a week in the bar of the late Mace's restaurant in the Pavilions shopping center. He ordered the same meal every time: a cup of soup, a small green salad and two glasses of Chardonnay. (I'm guessing his 2 p.m. meetings weren't on the peppy side.) He read the newspaper and greeted anyone who approached the beachhead he'd established.

One day we found ourselves, both alone, facing each other at our separate tables. I smiled, called out to him and gestured for him to join me, saying something inane like, "We're both by ourselves." He smiled and quietly said, "I know," and went back to his newspaper, soup, salad and wine. I learned a valuable lesson that day: I apparently have the capacity to embarrass myself in front of only myself. Check?

It is what it is (a win/win)

Just as the catch phrases "at the end of the day," "it is what it is" and "win/win" have over-ripened from overuse, "the elevator speech" has become ubiquitous in a number of sectors.

I'm sure you know what elevator speeches are and why they're called that. They're brief summaries of your product, cause or issue that can be delivered in the time it takes to ride up or down in a building. Effective elevator speeches can also be delivered between holes on a golf course and courses at a business dinner. They're ideal during lulls in the action at a Sacramento city council meeting (the biggest lull perhaps being the actual meeting).

The challenge with writing and delivering an elevator speech is that you never know how long that elevator ride is going to take. If you're riding down from the top floor of 555 Capitol Mall, you perhaps have enough extra time to stutter, whereas if your flight lasts only two floors, you can end up sounding like one of Alvin's chipmunks. Or like the guy who reads all of those disclaimers at the end of commercials for used car dealerships and erectile dysfunction products.

As a public service, I'd like to present an all-purpose elevator speech that you can adapt to your own needs:

"Hi. Hey, how 'bout those (name of a sports team everyone admires or body of elected officials no one's wild about, which may be redundant)?

"I couldn't help but notice that you got in on the same floor as I did. And I'll bet you'd also like to get in on the ground floor of a great new (product, cause or issue). I can tell because you feel the same way about the (team or elected

16

officials) as I do. What's that expression? 'Great minds like a think.'

"So here's the deal. If you'll give me your (business card, QR code or Social Security number), I'll send over some (promotional materials, product samples or exotic dancers) that I know you'll enjoy (reviewing, trying out or making a fool of yourself while thinking you're acting casual).

"Oops! Here's my (floor, destination or probation officer). I enjoyed our (chat, argument, fist fight) and hope you did, too. Have a (nice day, great afternoon, strong cocktail). I know I will (at the end of the day, because it is what it is or because just meeting you has been a win/win)."

Re-dress codes

The dress code in my office is pretty straightforward: I never wear one. That may sound a bit restrictive since I'm a company of one (who would I offend if I wore a comfy caftan at my desk, besides my cat?).

Yet my dress code apparently has nothing on the National Football League's, which just fined 49ers running back Frank Gore $10,500 "for wearing his socks too low" in the NFC Championship Game Jan. 20, as reported by Matthew Barrows in the Sacramento Bee.

This prompts five questions:

- If Gore had worn only one of his socks too low, would he have been fined only $5,250?
- What would the fine have been if he'd worn his socks at the correct height but, at closer inspection, they turned out to be mesh nylons?
- And as an important follow-up to that, what is the NFL's rule on wearing one's socks too high? There's a precedent for this kind of behavior. When I was in high school, a guy in my gym class showed up one day wearing a pair of panty hose on his head, the legs flopping all over like the Trix rabbit's ears. He was sent to the vice principal's office. So don't tell me this will never become an issue.
- What if Gore had worn no socks at all? Would he have been sued for emulating a Kardashian? If found guilty,

would he have been forced to star in a reality show with Bruce Jenner?

- By extension, can a business in another field now sue an employee for a similar infraction? If so, the whole notion of Casual Friday may be in jeopardy.

Well, at least there's a bright side to all of this.

CELEBRITIES I HAVE PRETENDED TO KNOW

Lunch with Kristine Hanson

A t 60, Kristine Hanson — TV and radio weather and sports reporter, master gardener, pet rescuer, impulsive bride and onetime Playboy Magazine centerfold — looks 35 and sounds 25. In a business that encourages jaded cynicism, she apparently didn't get the memo that dreams and optimism are supposed to fade with the first signs of age.

Over lunch with Hanson last week at Scott's Seafood, she updated me on what she's been up to since we last spoke, which was probably in 1977, when my late wife Jane was an on-air colleague at KCRA-TV.

First bombshell: She thinks she's pretty much done with her television career, which took her from Channel 3 to San Francisco's top-rated KGO-TV, and now sees her doing occasional climate prognosticating on Fox 40 news.

"I've loved TV, every minute and every day I've been in it," she says. "When I was doing the weather, I didn't have to be part of the rest of the operation. I had a windowless office where I gathered all the weather data and prepared the broadcast, all alone. Since the news directors never knew what I was talking about, they never interfered."

Hanson, who has a degree in meteorology from San Francisco State, was one of the first female weathercasters on TV. In 1977, three years after she posed for Playboy and two years after she joined KCRA, she received job offers — from stations in Philadelphia, Detroit, Boston, Chicago and San Francisco. She went with the latter, she says, "because how cool was it that I could still be close to my family and be in one of the most exciting cities in the country?"

She says another nice thing about being a weatherperson was, "Well, I love to talk. And what does everyone talk about? The weather." That has its occasional drawbacks. She recalls being snowed-in at a back-East airport years ago when "This elderly woman, with a cigarette dangling out of the side of her mouth, blamed the storm on the weathercasters. She said, 'These people are paid to be goddamned liars!' My husband at the time, Jim Fetzer, kept wanting to tell her I was a weathercaster but I stopped him. Why shouldn't the woman be able to blame someone for the delay?"

These days, in addition to her guest gigs on Channel 40, Hanson does fill-in work at a Santa Rosa adult contemporary radio station. She has homes in Healdsburg and Tahoe. She's thinking of combining her love for pets and gardening by opening a doggie day-care center and nursery at the same site. She'd certainly have no shortage of volunteers to water the geraniums.

Tomorrow: The second bombshell, or Kristine's four-day courtship.

Dec. 8, 2011

I wrote yesterday about a charming lunch I had last week with Kristine Hanson, the former weather and sports reporter for Sacramento's KCRA-TV and San Francisco's KGO-TV. She also was a Playboy Magazine centerfold in 1974, a fact that some columnists who share my name, address, height and DNA find difficult to ignore, especially because I still have that issue somewhere.

I ask Hanson if posing for the magazine helped or hurt her career. "Mainly, it helped," she says, "but not for the obvious reason that it brought me other modeling jobs. I got paid for being the centerfold and I was able to use that money to get through school. I was from a generation where

24

parents rarely could afford to pay for all their kids to go to college." Now 60 — but as I indicated yesterday, looking 35 and with the energy and dreams of someone who's 25 — Hanson has degrees in communication studies from Sac State and meteorology from San Francisco State.

I mentioned in Wednesday's clog that Hanson dropped two bombshells at lunch. The first was that she's not planning on staying in TV, even though she does occasional guest spots for Fox 40 news. Here's the second one: While she was doing weathercasting for a radio station in Santa Clara, she met her current husband as part of an on-air promotion.

"I'd mentioned that after going on so many bad dates through Match.com, I was now desperate to meet somebody nice and I was going to start trolling the airwaves for dates," she says. The station noticed that whenever Hanson was on the air and the talk turned to her romantic life, there was a corresponding spike in the ratings. It started playing less adult contemporary music and focused more on Hanson's adult contemporary life.

Eventually, listeners included a man named Robert Nicolas, with whom she went on a very public blind date to Train Town in Sonoma. Nicolas, who refurbishes and sells private planes for a living, proposed on that date — and married Hanson four days later.

"I wasn't even sure of his last name," Hanson says, laughing, "or what he liked to be called. To this day, my friends and I call him Robert-Bob, just to cover a couple of bases."

Secrets of model scout
Amber Collins

"Creative people sometimes have a hard time realizing they have to become CEOs of themselves," Amber Collins says after shimmying and gliding into a chair. This former model, who heads up the fashion division of Cast Images, a talent booking agency in midtown Sacramento, moves with the grace and confidence that launched her own 20-year modeling career when she was just 16.

Collins scouts, coaches and books mainly local talent for regional, national and global fashion shoots. She receives, she says, "more than 100 submissions a day," mostly from young people who have a dream of making it big in the industry — but who often don't realize how rare it is to be selected and how hard they need to work to build and sustain a career in front of the camera: "You can't sleep in, miss appointments and be difficult. Unless you're spectacular, honey, you just ain't worth the effort."

"It's been an interesting economy," Collins says, stirring the coffee she will mostly ignore during our chat. "We're still booking people left and right but we've found that in Sacramento, some people think the models will be provided for free in exchange for (their receiving) photos or visibility. People don't always realize that the event they're holding may not offer the be-all/end-all exposure that will enhance the careers of our models." She suggests that meeting planners "budget accordingly, including payment for models and other talent." She says she rarely encounters this conundrum when dealing with ad agencies and public relations firms. "They get it about being paid for services," she says.

I ask Collins to give some advice for readers of this column and publication who've taken good care of themselves and may harbor visions of nabbing a cool sideline — e.g., corporate raider by day, underpants mannequin by night. "Well, the first hoop is to follow the instructions on our website," she says. "I'm often amazed by people who show up for an open audition and don't bring photos of themselves or fill out the paperwork completely, even though we expressly tell them what to do before they arrive. My instant feeling is: If you can't take direction, you're not going to be a good client for us."

Not everyone even wants or needs to be a model, she admits. "I was with a friend of mine one weekend and we saw this great-looking guy in the supermarket," she recalls. "He was in his 40s, really fit, and had salt-and-pepper hair. A great look. You could just see him in a lifestyle ad, wearing chinos, a Polo shirt and running with his dog on the beach. We approached him. Turned out he was, like, a neurosurgeon. We didn't feel it was appropriate to ask, 'Would you mind quitting your day job to become a model?'"

On Monday, Collins tells all about body fat, supermodels and trends in the fashion industry. You'll want to dress for the occasion.

Feb. 6, 2012

On Friday I presented Part One of an action-packed chat with Amber Collins, the fashion director of Cast Images, the area's premier talent agency. Among her concerns as a professional and as a mom (she has an 11-year-old son named Cameron) is the plight of teenage girls who, to land modeling jobs, feel the need to pretend they're much younger and totally free of body fat and the curves acquired after adolescence.

Fashion designers, as I'm sure you've observed, often want runway and photo models to be skinny and shapeless. So they frequently employ 12- and 13-year-old girls, lavishly made up and eerily lighted, to model their clothes. "When these kids reach 16, they've usually gone through puberty," Collins says. "The only way they can hang onto their super-skinny, supermodel looks is by dieting. It's how they get anorexia and bulimia.

"That's why I'm glad they're starting to 'card' fashion models," she continues, "mainly in New York, to make sure they're at least 16. As New York goes, as far as in fashion, so goes the rest of the country — and maybe the world."

Collins tells me that modeling fees are lower today than they were as much as 10 years ago, owing to the economy. In addition, clients now demand unlimited usage of the photos (which can be negotiated in most cases). The upshot, though, is that models who accept a job posing for Ikea might find their pictures a year later in REI ads, for no additional compensation.

When I interviewed Collins in early 2011 for my late "Sacramentions" column in Sacramento Magazine, she told me she thought her son Cameron had real modeling potential (he's a handsome young man). No longer — or at least, not right now. "He's at that age where he doesn't want to spend time with his mom," she says with a sigh and a laugh. "I'm hoping that as he gets older and sees some of the very cute girls who work for me, he'll change his mind and start coming with me to fashion shoots."

Lucinda Chrisman: Dancing around the world

I t's rare when going along with the crowd could land you on the ground floor of what may become a pop phenomenon — but that's what filmmaker, actress and entrepreneur Lucinda Chrisman is banking on as she monitors the closing hours of an online campaign to raise funds for a TV series she's creating in Sacramento.

The show, "Around the World in 80 Dances," will be a musical travelogue, taking its host (Chrisman) to various spots on the planet to check out "their native dances, culture, food and fashion," she tells me the other afternoon as she sips hot tea at Peet's in midtown. Chrisman has been raising funds to shoot the first episode of the show — "which I'd rather not refer to as a pilot since I plan to shoot an entire season," she says — using a technique lately dubbed "crowd-funding" but which has been around since then-presidential candidate Howard Dean raised millions of dollars on the Internet. So far, her campaign website, 80dances.com, has attracted more than 80 donors. She hopes to make that 100 by 11:59 p.m. on Wednesday, Feb. 15, when her contract with the fundraising web host ends.

Whether she makes that goal or not, she already has $6,740 raised — well above the $4,000 she had sought online to add to other sources.

Originally from the South Bay Area, Chrisman has the striking looks, warm voice and effervescence of the best TV personalities. But she's also an award-winning film actor, a producer who's made a number of videos for clients such as Five Star Bank and Pfizer, and a confirmed world traveler.

Asked how she happened to alight in Sacramento about four years ago, her answer is reminiscent of Humphrey Bogart's (as Rick) in Casablanca when his friend asks him how he wound up in the desert city. Bogart says he came there for health purposes: specifically "for the waters." His friend (played by Claude Rains) points out that, being in an arid expanse, there are no waters. "I was misinformed," Bogart says (drily, we might add).

Chrisman says she came to California's capital "to look for fame and learn to surf," the latter part of that statement being the more amusingly preposterous. Then she gets serious. "I'm a businesswoman who travels," she says. "I wanted to be in a place that had a metropolitan airport, was right alongside I-5 and close to my mom's home (near Lake Oroville) and my nieces' in the Bay Area."

During the years she lived in Southern California, Chrisman took the occasional acting or dancing gig "in music videos, indie films and commercials" but says she simply didn't have "the fire in the belly to abandon my business every time I got a casting call." That business was a massage clinic she created and operated under the aegis of the California Healing Arts College in West Los Angeles, a few blocks from Santa Monica. Besides, she says, "As an actor, I was always expressing someone else's vision. I loved it but wanted to pursue my own."

Since her show is about dances native to various countries, the question arises about why she's shooting her first episode in Sacramento, where most of the dancing is done by elected officials at news conferences. "Oh," she exclaims, "don't you realize that West Coast swing originated in California? And that there are tons of fans of it here?"

I confess that I had no idea. But then, I've never gone along with the crowd.

Jennifer Whitney:
Anchor's away from TV

Before having coffee with her last week, the last time I'd seen Jennifer Whitney was at dinner in her elegant home in El Dorado Hills. At the time, she was probably the best-liked news anchor in town, with a mixture of glamorous looks, wide-open heart and a serious journalist's mind. Her husband, Bill Tucker, who owns Tucker Media Group, was a very funny host who clearly adored his wife and children: Carly, from his first marriage, who lived with the couple "from age 9 and on," Whitney says; and Willy, the couple's son together, who was a sweet-faced boy of about 11 or 12 at the time.

Things change. In 2006, Whitney became the victim of one of the TV industry's let's-change-things-up-for-no-apparent-reason purges, which sent her and her KOVR-TV Channel 13 co-anchor, the handsome and affable Paul Joncich, packing.

What many people don't realize is that a few months before she was let go, Whitney says, she had been offered the chance to stay on but under insultingly silly circumstances. At her request, and for a voluntary pay cut, she would be allowed to anchor only the 10 p.m. newscast (she wanted to spend more time with her family). But the station decreed she'd still need to come in during the 5 and 6 p.m. newscasts to "tease" her later broadcast (as in, "Coming up at 10: Many things you're already seeing at 5 and 6!"). That would have taken her all of a minute to do each time — after which she could either hang out at the station for four hours or trudge back to her home, 35 minutes away, then return by airtime. She resisted. The station said goodbye.

"It was very, very hard even though I'd seen it coming," Whitney says as she picks at a fruit cup in a midtown Java City. "I had done this for 20 years. After I left, I'd wake up in the morning and say out loud, 'What the hell am I going to do now?' I was scared." I ask if she also felt a sense of relief. "God, yes," she says. "Once I became an anchor, I rarely got to go out and report stories anymore. I sat in the studio. That was OK, in terms of the friendships I made, but I kept thinking I had more variety to offer. I still had some chapters in my life to explore."

Here are the things that either didn't change or changed for the better since that dinner. Jennifer and Bill have now been married 22 years ("He's my starter husband," she jokes). Little Willy is now a 6-foot-2-inch 19-year-old who plays wide receiver on a full football scholarship at Cal Poly San Luis Obispo. Bill's mother 90-year-old mom, Dottie Tucker, did not win $1 million in the lottery. And Whitney has embarked on a new career — as a marriage and family therapist.

Ah, but I see that our session's up for today. Let's pick it up from here tomorrow.

March 28, 2012

"I specialize in addiction," Jennifer Whitney says as she nibbles on a strawberry. No, this isn't a promo for an ABC After School Special or a group therapy confession. Well, maybe a little of the latter. For Whitney — after losing her anchor job at KOVR-TV Channel 13 in a housecleaning move when CBS took over the station — went back to school to become a marriage and family therapist.

"When I was a student at San Diego State, I was always torn between studying broadcast journalism or psychology," she says. "In the end, I graduated with a TV/radio emphasis." Yes, but in the epilogue, psychology won. "I'm doing exactly what I want to be doing," she says.

What she wants to do, and now does, is go back and forth between both the worlds that fascinate her. Using her married name of Tucker in her professional practice, she hosts (as Whitney) a regular radio show on mental health Saturday mornings at 8 on KSTE-AM 650, an outgrowth of Prop. 63's "Free Your Mind!" project, a public service show sponsored by the Los Angeles County Department of Mental Health. She's appearing in a documentary on mental health. She sees patients, mostly from the El Dorado Hills/Folsom area-and to stay in shape, she runs and teaches spinning classes at a couple of gyms.

"I am much more relaxed," she says. "But I guess what I miss most about TV, besides the people, is the access it gave me. I don't mean that self-important kind of access: 'I'm from the media, you must take my call.' I mean the kind that lets you get right to the person making decisions, so you can help someone or tell the story with authority. I think of myself as a story-teller."

She then tells me a doozy. For a Christmas present this past year, her family bought her husband Bill's 90-year-old mother, Dottie Tucker, lottery "scratchers." Because Dottie had accidentally over-scratched a losing 8 to look like a winning 6, the ticket at first appeared to be worth $1 million. "It was interesting to see how Dottie's winning the money affected everyone else," Whitney says. You'd expect a psychology student to say this, of course.

The wizardly wonder who's Oz

D r. Mehmet Oz complimented me on my biceps yesterday morning — and I have witnesses! In case you've missed the hue and hoopla surrounding the Emmy-winning talk show host's appearance in Sacramento, Oz and his wife of 27 years, Lisa, were here to launch HealthCorps, a nonprofit effort to battle childhood obesity by enlisting young people into a mentoring/ monitoring effort at the high school level. (Its business model is none other than the Peace Corps.) The couple is on a nationwide fundraising tour and, Oz tells me, estimates that a fundraiser scheduled for last evening at Memorial Auditorium was likely to raise "around $2 million." Surely not from the expected gate receipts, I suggest. "Oh no, I'm talking about sponsorships, big sponsorships, major corporations, individuals," he says in the same rapid-fire cadence he displays on his TV show. (To find out more, you can visit healthcorps.org or text HEALTH at 20222.)

In person, Dr. Oz is, if possible, even more energetic than he appears on his program, which airs here weekdays on KCRA-TV Channel 3. A bit over six feet tall and aggravatingly trim, he's wearing a handsome dark suit and tie instead of his trademark scrubs or blazer/slacks combo as he and Lisa — who's petite, dark-haired and movie-star pretty — slide out of their driver's car. Both are down-to-earth and unfailingly polite to the staff at the midtown restaurant Mulvaney Building & Loan, where we're ushered into a small private room for a chat.

Both are also pumped about the get-together they'd had that morning with students at Hiram Johnson High School. "These kids were so excited because they know that

34

my vision isn't that curing obesity will promise them better health, make them look better and all of that. The program's about developing an awareness of what they put in their bodies — and that if they can learn to control that, it can lead to their becoming successful in other aspects of their lives."

"A lot of these kids don't even know how to read a food label," Lisa Oz, an author in her own right, says. "We're teaching them the need to move around more and to develop a mental resilience. What they're really learning is how to make decisions."

I ask the couple if there are a few basic rules that can help a busy businessperson get and/or stay in shape without having to hire personal trainers, life coaches, private chefs and a staff who'll constantly tell him or her, "You look fabulous today, Boss." The good doctor takes that one. He's developed a 10-minute stretching/seven-minute exercise program that involves sit-ups and pushups. "Once I do that every morning, I can go all day long guilt-free because I know I already exercised," he says.

Oz also says that having breakfast every day ("And I don't mean Pop Tarts") is essential — and that having the exact same breakfast is important. "I personally like blueberries and yogurt," he says. His consuming passion, one might say, is for nuts. "Nuts are the life force of the universe," he says. "Trees grow from nuts. Nuts grow on trees."

He recommends eating some "a half-hour before lunchtime. It's quick and easy and keeps you from overeating." He also calls 3-4 p.m. "the bewitching hour ... you don't want to make any important decisions then. You only have so much decision-making potential in one day. Being in shape is about energy management, not time management. Know your own body."

Ed Goldman: But I Digress ...

That's when he says the thing about my biceps, which are far less impressive than my lifelong ability to buy suits with sleeves that are far too thin. This is called decision-making.

Beth Ruyak: Behind the microphone

A frightening number of years ago, I did a small media tour when my first book, "How To Incorporate Your Dog (And Other Solid Business Tips)," came out. One of my stops was Channel 3's Noon News, which is how I met today's special guest star, Beth Ruyak. She was co-anchoring the broadcast with the late Mike Boyd. When it came time to interview me on the set, Ruyak absolutely floored me with the introduction to her first question: "As I was reading your book last night ..." I can't entirely recall what followed. I simply couldn't get beyond the fact that a host had actually read the book an author was plugging on her show.

"Guests deserve the research we do on them or their topics before they come on our shows," she says the other morning during a de-briefing immediately following her Capital Public Radio program, "Insight." Her producers, Jen Picard and James Morrison, are not only courteous to me but also completely unconcerned that I may jot down a trade secret or two as they and Ruyak review the hour-long program that just aired and discuss the next day's lineup of guests.

Of course, nothing has gone wrong on the show. Oh, one guest apparently thought he'd been hired to do a 10-minute monologue (in a monotone, no less), but the only near-calamity might have been that Ruyak was fighting a cold. (She even slips in a quick impersonation of Marlene Dietrich when chatting with guest commentator Jeff Hudson.)

Ruyak has been hosting "Insight" since April. The show airs live on Monday through Friday from 10-11 a.m. five days a week, and is repeated in the evening. While she tells me she's "very grateful to have a job," she's never been out of work for very long. In addition to her time at Channel 3, she's reported on (and from) the Olympics for KCRA's parent network, NBC several times.

Ruyak says she keeps herself in shape these days by "running in a swimming pool. That sounds strange, huh? But that's what I do, ever since I injured my knee." I look at her — slender, energetic and slightly past the half-century mark — and write down Note to Self: Buy Waterproof Sneakers.

Tomorrow: How Ruyak turned from shy tomboy to semi-choreographer. Please tune in.

Sept. 19, 2012

Despite its being one of the most overused words in the English language, I have to say that "authentic" is the adjective that best describes Beth Ruyak. Not only for me but also for the millions of TV viewers who've watched her during her 30-year career in broadcasting — and today, the many thousands of listeners who tune in her Capital Public Radio show "Insight" every morning. How authentic? "I'm 51," she says when I ask. As you know, not too many media people — or for that matter, other professionals of a certain age — like revealing their ages.

Off the air, Ruyak is almost exactly the same as she is in front of her microphone — friendly, direct and curious. How curious? She asks me so many questions about my life and career during our interview that I have to keep reminding her, but mainly me, that she's the subject.

She didn't start out this way. "I was a complete tomboy," she says. "I didn't know how to dress, how to put on make-up or even why I was supposed to put on make-up." A modeling class in high school started turning her around, she says. Not long thereafter, "I accidentally won a beauty contest. I mean,

I wasn't supposed to be in it, it just kind of....." Her voice trails off, though she's grinning at the memory.

When I suggest to Ruyak that in my limited encounters with her she's struck me as a recovering shy person, she gets very quiet — so quiet that I think I've offended her. But no. "Nobody knows that about me," she says. "But yes, it was a struggle to come out of that when I was younger. I think what saved me was I always liked telling stories — and that's really what journalists do. A lot of my work has been about reaching out from shyness."

Though she doesn't use the word, Ruyak sees her job as being as much a choreographer as an interviewer. "It's a dance," she says, "to know when to cut in (during an interview) and when to let the other person lead." Since Ruyak took over the show in April, Capital Public Radio has received a complaint — "Exactly one," her senior producer, Jen Picard, tells me — because Ruyak had interrupted an interviewee who perhaps didn't realize that a dialogue is supposed to involve two people.

Ruyak writes her own scripts (the introductions, the general framework and tone of the questions she wants to ask) and sends them to the Capital Public Radio staff around 6:30 a.m. Monday through Friday. Responding to the obvious follow-up question, she says, "I, uh, get up around 4:30 each day. That's crazy, isn't it, considering that the show doesn't start until 10 a.m.?" For a split second, she actually seems embarrassed by her work ethic. Or maybe just a little shy.

TOIL, TROUBLE AND TRAVEL

While House foils terrorist tourists

With a new TV show about terrorism premiering any second, I've been thinking about a trip to Washington DC that my wife and I made last spring.

We went for a few reasons — to visit her nephew, who was about to graduate from the U.S. Naval Academy in Annapolis; to allow me to interview Congresswoman Doris Matsui just as the government was about to shut down (spoiler alert: it didn't); and because, well, I'd never been to my nation's capital.

Matsui's office arranged for Candy and me to tour the White House one morning at 8 a.m. We rose early, Candy grabbed her purse and we walked the mile or so from our hotel to 1600 Pennsylvania Ave.

"Grabbed her purse" is the key phrase here. For when we arrived at the guardhouse, one of the armed, uniformed men told the unarmed, uninformed us that no bags were permitted on the grounds. "Where can we go to check my wife's purse?" I asked with the no-nonsense tone of the veteran globe-trotter. The armed, uniformed fellow — perhaps suppressing a laugh and/or the understandable desire to call me a cretin — said there was no baggage desk at the White House, that we'd have to take the purse back to our hotel room. It was now 7:45 a.m.

One thing my wife and I are pretty good at is realizing when there's really no point in discussing options with armed, uniformed guys. We bolted from the gate and ran across the street into the lobby of the Willard Hotel. We made for the concierge's desk and asked what he'd charge us to check Candy's purse for an hour or so. The concierge

— perhaps suppressing a laugh and/or the understandable desire to call me a cretin (or did I already use that phrase?) — said that, due to Homeland Security restrictions, the only way we could check the bag was if we were registered guests at the hotel.

"Let me get this straight," said the cretin wearing my clothes: "If I checked into the hotel and we happened to have an explosive device in our totes, that'd be all right?"

The concierge smiled indulgently and I was glad he wasn't armed. "That's one way of looking at it," he said, adding he hoped we were enjoying our visit to the capital, this being Cherry Blossom time.

The upshot of the story is that we walked briskly outside (running would have sent the wrong signal at this point, we decided). I used my best New York voice to hail a cab instead of waiting for the hotel doorman to slowly consider doing so and we got back to the hotel. It was now 7:55 a.m.

While I entertained the cabbie with a rollicking recap of our day so far — to which I'm certain he only feigned indifference (and that he spoke no English) — Candy flew upstairs, dropped off her purse, flew back down, hopped in the taxi and away we rode. Amazingly, we got back to the White House by 8:15 a.m. and the armed, uniformed man escorted us inside with courtesy, dispatch and perhaps a giggle. Candy thought he just had allergies. After all, it was Cherry Blossom time.

June 15, 2012

Escape to New York

I just returned from spending a week on the exotic little island where I was born, Manhattan. It was my first trip back in more than 25 years. I didn't go back to visit any relatives. My uncles, aunts, in-laws and outlaws are long gone — some to their graves, a few to gated communities in Miami and, for all I know, one or two to Attica, another gated community.

Until I was 8, I lived in the Bronx in a one-square-mile apartment complex of 100 eight- and 12-story brick buildings called Parkchester. It was built under Pres. Franklin Delano Roosevelt's Works Progress Administration well before I was born. So much for my superhero origins.

New York has changed since I was a kid, though not nearly as much as people who claim to be nostalgic for the years when it was dangerous to stroll in Times Square after midnight will tell you, with macho regret. To be sure, it does feel a little safer these days. But I'd still advise you to leave your bling in the hotel safe, to keep your eyes open and to refrain from making pithy cultural observations.

While this really is the city that doesn't sleep, I somehow managed to sleep just fine through the all-night construction, car honking and street-corner choral groups — possibly because I have three neighbors in Sacramento currently remodeling their homes (though not in the middle of the night).

It was pointed out to me that every night is trash night in Manhattan. As I watched workers loading immense plastic bags of the stuff into stegosaurus-sized trucks, I recalled that when I was a kid, the city's garbage workers went on strike for a few days, crippling the city because those abandoned curbside bags made it impossible to travel certain narrow streets. It was early winter and the snow had also turned to slush, making even walking difficult. (This situation might also have occurred some years earlier, in 1944. That's when lyricists Adolph Green and Betty Comden called the city "a helluva town.")

If you'll indulge me just a little longer, on Monday, I'll tell you what it was like to visit not only the city of my birth but the actual community, building and apartment in which I lived. I'm still a little peeved that in the decades since I left, no one's put up a historical marker that says "Ed Goldman Slept Here." On the other hand, I'm not sure how much sleep I actually got back then. It was a pretty noisy neighborhood — but at least none of my neighbors was remodeling.

June 18, 2012

D uring my recent week in New York, I had set aside a couple of hours to visit 1561 Metropolitan Ave., the Bronx apartment building in which I spent the first eight years of my (wisely) unexamined life. It's in Parkchester, a one-square-mile community of 100 nearly identical brick buildings that was built under Pres. Franklin D. Roosevelt's WPA program.

My parents allowed my brothers and me, at pretty early ages, to head downstairs to the playground unaccompanied. People simply didn't kidnap the children of firefighters since no one would have been able to afford to pay the ransom, except in benefits. Besides, there were always cops walking the beat (there still are) and you could always find somebody's parents sitting on nearby benches. I think there was a tacit understanding among them that any parent could yell at you for going down the slide headfirst. A potential kidnapper would have been tackled and arrested before he could pull a tempting lollipop out of his coat.

But you could still get lost easily in this maze of lookalike apartment houses, particularly if you were a kid like me who believed he was Kit Carson, his tricycle was a horse and the endless expanse of concrete and brick was mountains and plains. That's why one of the first things I was taught to say was my building address and apartment number, "3-F, as in Frank." I had a slight lisp and my mom wasn't taking any chances of my being taken to somebody else's place.

I'm sure you've had the experience of revisiting your childhood home or neighborhood and, if they were still standing, noting that everything seemed somehow smaller. This wasn't the case for me, with one exception. In the winter, we used to ride our sleds down a snow-covered hillock that contained a few embedded stones. We ominously referred to the area as The Rocks, and begged our parents to allow us to go there. Permission would be granted with seeming hesitation though I'm sure I turned back too swiftly once and caught my parents winking at each other. Apparently, the danger was either minimal or nonexistent — though anyone who's ever been, known or had a kid knows that children can find ways to injure themselves, even playing checkers. In fact, letting them go down a slide headfirst may be safer.

Surcharges worth paying

The New York Times ran a piece in its Travel section last Sunday about the multitude of hidden fees charged by airlines and hotels — which I'm sure came as a huge surprise to anyone who has neither traveled nor stayed in a hotel for the past decade.

"There are now charges for reservations, cancellations, boarding early, departing early, holding bags, checking bags and using the gym, business center and the safe in your room," we were informed. It got me to thinking — which, if you read this column every so often, realize is a rare and miraculous thing — about some of the things we don't get charged for but would probably be willing to:

- I would pay to not hear the what-to-do-in-case-of-emergency speech that precedes each flight. Not because the information, if edited, isn't useful, but because sometimes it's offered to the point of comedy. Example: My flight back to Sacramento from Orange County a few weeks ago was delayed, then extended so that Southwest could drop some passengers off in Oakland on the way (their flights had been rerouted due to bad weather in Phoenix and Las Vegas). So we boarded the plane, heard the emergency speech and flew to Oakland, where we dropped off those passengers and didn't pick up any new ones (remember that part). We now faced a brisk 15-minute flight to Sacramento during which we'd never climb above 10,000 feet and would be able to see the ground the entire time. Nonetheless, the flight attendant again told passengers who'd heard the speech only an hour before what to do in case of a "water landing." A guy sitting across the aisle from me — who had displayed a serious devotion to beer on the first flight — blurted out, "Yeah, like if we land in somebody's pool!"

- I would also consider paying a surcharge to be able to actually hear what the pilot is saying when his voice comes on over the speakers with all the clarity of a high school kid mumbling back my order at a drive-through burger place. Perhaps the airlines could use super-titles, as is done at the opera to translate librettos, or install closed captioning, as is done for people with hearing disabilities. Perhaps the pilot could be required to take diction lessons. Perhaps I'll disguise myself when I fly again.

- If the hotels wished me to pay extra to ensure that the housekeeping staff didn't maintain a running dialogue at 6 a.m. — from far-flung rooms and throughout the hallways — I'd do it without hesitation. In advance.

Traveling to L.A., Mars — What's the difference?

National Public Radio reported last week that a test to see how people might handle a round trip to Mars revealed that some of them were very tired by the end of their simulated 17-month space voyage in cramped quarters. This led to the startling conclusion that some people might be better suited to take a trip to Mars than other people. I'm definitely one of those other people.

I've driven round trips to Los Angeles from Sacramento more times than I care to remember. I realize that L.A. is no Mars — or at least it's not as far away as Mars — and I'm guessing my car was a tad more comfortable than a space capsule. In addition, when I drove to L.A. on I-5, I could always stop at Harris Ranch for a truly fresh hamburger (you pass by acres of cows just before you reach the restaurant; it's not as immediate as selecting your lobster entree from a tank as you glide to your table, but a bit unsettling nonetheless.)

Sometimes, when my daughter was little and her bladder was apparently microscopic, we'd take Highway 99 to L.A. That route added almost an hour to the drive but allowed us to stop every 45 minutes or so in a town, where we could find a park in which she could run around and exhaust herself for about 20 minutes, or a town in which we could buy a souvenir (how many of you have a cup from the Perko's Coffee Shop in Taft — and am I turning you emerald with envy?)

I loved my family but hated, hated, hated the drive. Every time I drove down there, the same thing happened.

I'd assume we'd been logging some serious miles and that at any moment I'd see a sign telling us L.A. was a mere 50 miles ahead. Instead, I'd sneak a glance at a sign and find I hadn't even reached Stockton.

This is when I began to seriously consider beginning the practice of Zen or developing an addiction to Prozac — anything that could put me into a still-alert, altered state that would make me at one with the car. Or whatever.

When we'd return from the trip, I found I could doze for 12 hours. The only thing that interrupted me — with a terrible start — was I'd dream I was still behind the wheel and had fallen asleep. I guess that would be allowed on a trip to Mars, though.

Here's to the all-seeing TSA

Dear Transportation Security Administration:
Please disregard my recent employment
application. It has just come to my attention, via an
Associated Press story, that you are discontinuing the use of
highly revealing body scanners at the nation's airports.

I had been looking forward to my interview, two or three
follow-up interviews and maybe a few demonstrations of the
scanners after my being hired — you know, for my employee
orientation session.

It grieves me to withdraw my application, but candor
demands that I explain why, in detail — though certainly
not the level of detail I had been hoping to encounter at that
employee orientation session.

To be sure, I was never clear on why the scanners
needed to reveal so many facets of a passenger's body.
Are there data suggesting that especially hunky men or
appealingly curvy women pose greater or lesser threats to
our country's security? I'll admit that both types pose threats
to my own sense of security, which may be why I'm usually
cited as the most overdressed occupant in my health club's
locker room.

Are most terrorists tubby? Are most skinny? Do they
wear X-ray-obvious toupees or misleading cosmetic add-
ons?

I know you've said that the peek-a-boo scanners you're
retiring produced images that couldn't be stored (nor,
presumably, uploaded to YouTube) and that the security
worker who looked at the images wasn't allowed to have
any interaction with the passengers he or she had been
scrutinizing. I'm sure it was just a coincidence when a TSA

worker smirked at me after I'd undergone a scanning at
an out-of-town airport. Perhaps she'd just heard a funny
remark.

On the other hand, maybe her tummy was upset — and
what I took to be a smirk was actually a belch in progress.
Just to be on the safe side, maybe you should have somebody
at TSA scan her.

Best wishes for your future success,

Ed Goldman

(The guy with the — well, you already know)

A modest proposal
for Southwest Airlines

Boarding an airplane these days takes longer than some of the flights.

I'm not talking about the TSA cavity searches or nude photography (Pardon. I mean body-scan imaging). I'm referring to how long it takes to find a seat while people attempt to shove vanloads of clothing into the plane's overhead storage bins.

On a recent trip to Austin, which they keep in Texas, we managed to score pretty good pole positions in the Southwest Airlines boarding queue: A-33 and A-34. But as we left the terminal and walked down the corridor to the plane, human traffic started to back up worse than an I-80 commute from Sacramento to Roseville at 5 p.m.

The reason, of course, is that the people who preceded us, already on the plane, had chosen seats in the first few aisles of the plane, presumably so they could land in Austin earlier than we would. In so doing, they brought the boarding procedure to a standstill as they jammed what looked like steamer trunks into bins capable of holding at most a tote, a briefcase and an undernourished cat.

There's a remedy for this madness, and I hope someone at Southwest is not only listening but also knows someone on the Nobel Peace Prize committee. I'd even settle for a MacArthur Foundation genius grant.

Why can't Southwest simply have passengers enter from the rear of the plane? They could rush down the aisle and still grab the front seats — but they'd schlep their luggage with them and bother no one as they fumbled, heaved and exhorted their "carryons" to fit in the storage bins.

I know what you're thinking: What about those people who board early so they can claim seats toward the middle or even back of the plane? Wouldn't they cause the same pile-up whether they entered from the front or back?

No. Not if the airlines would tell them to sit the hell down, shut the hell up and start checking their stupid bags curbside.

Why do the skies have to be so friendly, anyway?

ENTREPRENEURS
AND OTHER SUPERHEROES

Feb. 9, 2012

Meet Wikipedia's Jimmy Wales

"**D**on't be sneaky," says Jimmy Wales, founder of Wikipedia. That's his advice to public relations people who try to get client messages onto the open-content website that sprang to life and straight into controversy 11 years ago. The nonprofit online encyclopedia — which its founder admits "has had some verification issues in the past" — currently houses nearly four million articles.

"It's made me unhappy when we've made an error," Wales tells me. "But it's never made me cry. It's motivated us. We always go back and figure out what we did wrong — and more to the point, how to make sure we never do it again."

Wales is wearing a black mock-turtleneck sweater, black slacks, black shoes and a formless grayish blazer. He looks stylish (if truth be told, I dress very much the same way and am still not rich) but also as though he doesn't pay a lot of attention to looking fashion-forward (ditto!). He sports black horn-rimmed glasses, has dark, receding hair and perhaps to appear au courant but more likely because he's exhausted from traveling, has a 5 o'clock shadow — or at least it was 30 minutes before our 5:30 p.m. chat at the Fairmont Hotel, immediately prior to his speech to roughly 100 eager students at Hult International Business School's San Francisco campus.

I ask Wales if he thinks that Wikipedia's recent publicity-grabbing blackout did any good. You'll recall that many websites — including Wikipedia — shut down for 24 hours on Jan. 18 to protest Congress' latest, and typically over-the-top, bid to institute anti-piracy laws on the web. I should point out here that Vice President Joe Biden, who's president of the U.S. Senate, has plagiarized speeches and been caught doing it; it's not all that relevant to this issue but, as a writer who's been pilfered from more than a few times, I never want anyone to forget it. Thank you for your patience.

The two bills that Wales and his compatriots were protesting, on the grounds that they were what Wales and others call "draconian," were the Senate's Stop Online Piracy Act, or SOPA, and the House of Representatives' Protect Intellectual Property Act, or PIPA. This may be the only time you've seen the words "congress" and "intellectual" in the same story.

"I think it was a huge success," Wales says. "SOPA and PIPA have been completely shelved. Darrell Issa says the issues are radioactive now." Issa, a Republican, is the U.S. Representative for California's 49th congressional district, which includes Vista, a city in North San Diego County. I know this because I looked it up on, yes, Wikipedia. My fact checkers are standing by.

As a parting shot, I ask Wales — whose cool name makes him sound like a Scottish rock star — if he'll ever launch a blackout again. "Oh, I hope not," he says calmly. Then he shrugs. "But then again, history has yet to be written." Now, that's sneaky.

Meet future biz superstar Manpreet Kaur

A t 23, Rancho Cordova resident Manpreet Kaur already owns and leases out more than a few residential properties in the Sacramento area through her company, EZ Stop Real Estate. She earned her bachelor's degree in managerial economics from the University of California Davis and has been working 24/7 toward a master's degree in international business this August from the San Francisco campus of Hult International Business School.

To give you an idea of Kaur's academic prowess, I should mention that Hult has five campuses around the world, that it requires students to pay their full tuition up front, that only 15 percent of its student body hails from the United States and that it went after her.

Kaur, who was born in the state of Punjab, India, is currently the only student at Hult from this region. She came to the U.S. with her parents when she was 8. She graduated from Rocklin High School and spent two years at Sierra College (also in Rocklin) before heading to UC Davis, from which she graduated in 2010.

"I've loved my time at Hult," she says, "because the focus is on team projects, on gaining practical knowledge. The school only has a few classrooms-but also 30 or 40 breakout rooms for the teams to meet in."

As a result, catching up with Kaur was a little like scheduling a chat with a head of state. We finally speak the day after she and her team have presented a marketing plan they created for an event-planning firm not far from the

61

campus, ZeroCater. "The master's program is only a year long, so you work very, very hard," she says.

Kaur says her age can sometimes prove to be a barrier in her business dealings. "The banks might say that my age doesn't matter to them because look at my (portfolio), but it's an underlying problem for them," she says. In December, Kaur incorporated her real estate business. "Now they'll be dealing with my tax i.d. number, not with someone who's 23."

I ask Kaur what she hopes to do after she graduates from Hult. "This is where it gets really intense," she says. "In today's times, it's not in your best interest to focus on only one thing. We must excel in many areas, which is why I've tried to have many paradigms underneath me — business, economics, administration, real estate, marketing. Real estate will never be my main business. It isn't something that requires my attention full-time once I've bought a property and leased it out." When she tells me she "wouldn't mind getting a Ph.D. after working for a few years," I ask if she'd consider teaching.

"Oh, I like learning too much," she says. "I'm much more of a student than a teacher." Make that an A-plus student.

Oct. 11, 2012

Last March I interviewed a remarkable young woman, Manpreet Kaur, by phone — something I rarely do for this column because getting out and meeting people not only provides a fuller depiction of them, but is also more fun.

At the time, Kaur, who currently lives with her parents and much younger brother in Rancho Cordova, was 23 years old, finishing up her masters in international business at the San Francisco campus of Hult University and, on the side, leasing out several residential properties she owned. Getting together in person would have demanded the timing of a military sortie so we contented ourselves with a phone interview and follow-up emails.

A couple of weeks ago she contacted me and we scheduled three in-person chats that I kept needing to postpone. We finally connected on Tuesday of this week — and am I glad we did. First, let me state the obvious reason: She's a very pretty, self-confident young woman, with one of the most direct speaking styles I've ever encountered in one so young (she turned 24 on Sept. 2). Second: Her take on the Sacramento job market, based on having gone through a battery of interviews (and an offer or two) takes me by such surprise that if I weren't sitting across from her at a Starbucks off Zinfandel Drive, I might have assumed her pronouncements are satirical. But despite having an easy, tuneful laugh, she is in dead earnest about the experiences she's been racking up.

"Employers here don't understand that they can leverage young people like me," she says. "We have new ideas. Everyone talks about the need for Americans to innovate — well, young people are able to innovate. We aren't locked into the same old way of doing things. Leverage us!"

Companies in San Francisco, she says, "really focus on young people. In Sacramento, it's all about, 'How much experience do you have?'"

On the day of our chat, Kaur is on her way to her fourth interview with a major communications company. "I had told them that one of the things I excelled at when I was a student was doing presentations," she says. "So the person interviewing me says, 'OK, show us.' I said I'd be back in an hour. I went home, looked at my notes from a presentation I'd made on hotel renovations — obviously, not relevant to this company, but one I was comfortable making — and got back there in 45 minutes." The potential employer brought "about nine managers and line people" into a conference room and Kaur did her thing. It went over well, she recalls.

When I suggest to her that having four interviews for the same job — and being given the chance to meet people she'll likely be working with — seems, to me at least, that the company is interested in her, she sighs and smiles. "I worry about coming off as arrogant," she says.

Maybe over the phone. In person, never.

Terry Foley knows what's in a name

Terry Foley is what you might call the master of many domains. He creates, owns, buys, leases, brokers and sells Internet names for companies and nonprofits. "I help businesses brand themselves," he says over coffee near his home in East Sacramento. "I ask people, 'What do you do? What are you thinking of calling yourself?' And the most important question I ask them is, 'Why?'"

He says that while there are exceptions — like "Google," a word that used to mean nothing but now is a noun, a verb and an empire — the best domain names are related to an organization's mission. "'You sell dog food?' I might ask. 'OK. Let's see if we can get that into your domain name,'" he says. "I'm usually at my best with cause-and-effect names."

As an example, Foley (you can reach him at qpone@ hotmail.com) mentions a few of his recent creations: theaterbuffs.com, which has a clearly defined audience (an audience!); saconthecheap.com; and the concept he hopes a city or sports booster will talk to him about buying or leasing in the next few months, USSeniorOpenSacramento. That namesake tournament is headed here in 2015.

Even when people don't immediately rush to buy one of Foley's dozens of names, he can realize revenue by "parking" the name with a company, such as one called SEDO, that creates a page for the name and then attracts relevant businesses to advertise on the content-light website.

Here's how this works: Let's say I create the domain name for a (nonexistent) French restaurant called, oh, "Chez It Isn't So." I park the domain name (chezitisntso.com) with the SEDO people, who send out the word about the name's existence. Winemakers, travel-abroad agencies, language tutors and other restaurants ask to have their link added to the site. "Every time someone clicks on one of those links, I make money," Foley says.

An event planner who brought big names to speak at local Borders book stores for several years, Foley wants his next big project to celebrate Sacramento, which he loves (he's lived in only two houses, within blocks of each other, for most of his 56 years).

One would be a website called goodforce.org, which funders and local entrepreneurs can visit to exchange ideas. The other would be a "walk of stars" similar to Hollywood's celebrity street tributes, and other displays, which would honor "the people who've helped put Sacramento on the map."

He mentions Alexandra ("Ray") Eames, who — with her husband Charles Eames — designed some of the last century's most iconic furniture. "Can't you picture a gigantic Eames chair on a sidewalk or in a park here?" says Foley. Bet he has a domain name all set to go.

What Jack Crawford is up to

Jack Crawford Jr. made a life-altering decision when he was working on an MBA degree at the University of California Davis. He dropped out. "A venture capitalist had told me he'd fund a business I was developing, but only if I could pay full attention to running it — in other words, if I wasn't going to school when I should be devoting every moment to the business. It wasn't that tough a choice."

Nor the wrong one, apparently. Crawford, who's 45, is the general partner of Velocity Venture Capital. The company has helped fund some notable startups in the region, including Laru Corp. and Revionics. He says that while Revionics has cadged its share of ink (it was featured in a story in the Business Journal this past May when the tech firm was named a finalist for a major national award), Laru is poised for growth. "You're going to hear more and more about this company in the next 12-18 months," he promises.

That's not surprising. Laru offers risk and compliance management software apps to financial institutions — a few of which, you might have heard, have found it difficult to pay attention the past few years.

Last month, Crawford's Folsom-based firm hosted the first meeting of its Entrepreneurs Showcase, a six-month program that shows up-and-coming businesspeople how to develop funding pitches. Two hundred people attended to soak up advice from investors from Dell, Samsung and Oracle, as well as the keynote address by Mark Heesen, president of the National Venture Capital Association.

On Sept. 27, Velocity will hold its second meeting, at the Sacramento Convention Center. Its theme, Crawford says, is "learning how to focus on and take advantage of the financing food chain."

Crawford says he believes that Sacramento "is a great place to build companies — but if you want to scale them for growth, you need to look through the telescope a little more than a lot of people do." He points to the Silicon Valley as being "an easy day trip. You need to go down there and develop relationships with VCs. I want to build a bridge between our two valleys."

Crawford points out that the Silicon Valley and Boston are "the two major hubs for venture capitalists in the United States. You can find 42 percent of all of the VCs in the country there."

Ah, but how many of them were smart enough to drop out of their MBA programs?

Christopher Johnson
uses his noodles

For Christopher Johnson, instant meals just aren't instant enough. That's why he's invented the Rapid Ramen noodle bowl. The device more than halves the time needed to prepare Top Ramen, the college dorm favorite that's also consumed by gazillions of people around the world every day.

Walmart is piloting the square bowl at its Truxel Road store this fall, Johnson says. Since Top Ramen packages have never mentioned using a microwave to prepare the noodles, Rapid Ramen comes with complete nuking instructions.

"I'm not moved by fear or obstacles," Johnson tells me over coffee at House Kitchen & Bar, the restaurant on the first floor of 555 Capitol Mall. From his office upstairs he runs a budding fiefdom, which includes his self-named basketball academy, a corporate recruiting firm (The Johnson Group) and, of course, his Rapid Ramen enterprise.

Johnson, 33, began his recruiting business when he was 26. "The business model is unusual," he says. "Instead of working on a job-by-job basis, we have yearly contracts with a number of companies. We're more like employees than consultants. It provides consistency." He says the company posted $1 million in revenues over a recent 18-month period.

He's pursuing patents on at least three additional inventions — two of his own and one that his wife, Shawna, is working on. For understandable proprietary reasons, he won't discuss the products in detail, but allows that they're in the fields of sports equipment, hair care and children's toys.

Johnson has the graceful lope of a basketball player, a sport he played in school and which he now coaches. He's been in love with Shawna ("who runs all of my companies' back offices," he says) since he was 14 years old. The couple, married 11 years, has three children: sons Chris, 13 ("who looks just like me"), and Josiah, 9 ("who is me!"), and four-year-old daughter Chloe. The family lives in Wilton. This summer, Johnson was one of four local men to be named a named a Father of the Year by the Father's Day Council.

At our coffee, Johnson presents me with my very own Rapid Ramen noodle bowl, then emails me the directions that will be included in the package once it's ready for prime time. The directions are quite clear. But I don't follow directions well. Tomorrow, I'll reveal how it cost me close to $200 to test a bowl that will retail for $5.99.

Sept. 7, 2012

Yesterday I told you about Christopher Johnson, a 33-year-old business dynamo who's just invented the Rapid Ramen noodle bowl, a device that Walmart will test-market at its Truxel Road store this fall. Today I'll show you how NOT to use the $5.99 product — unless you're willing to spend close to $200.

At my local Rite-Aid store, I bought a package of eight Top Ramen dehydrated soup mixes for less than $1.50. I took it home and used up three of the mixes trying to follow instructions for cooking them in the Rapid Ramen bowl, which are easy to follow if you're anyone but me.

I used up the first pack because I didn't put enough water in the bowl. The second time I used too much water and left it in the microwave so long that even with the bowl's heat-resistant handles, I scalded my fingertips removing it from the oven — because of the overflowing radiated water,

70

not the bowl itself, which remained at room temperature on the outside.

The third time went like a charm. I found, as Johnson had claimed, that because less water is required to microwave than to boil Top Ramen, I needed to use only half of the enclosed seasoning — a good thing since each Top Ramen seasoning pack contains the recommended daily sodium intake of an emerging nation.

You may be wondering about the "close to $200" remark. Apparently, in a burst of technological know-how, I shoved the two uneaten but nuked batches of noodle soup down my sink, then turned on the garbage disposal. On Labor Day, a very nice fellow named Dave Eline of Shoreline Plumbing, based in Roseville, came by and, as he restored the function of my disposal, sink and ability to reason, he gently lectured me on the only items one should ever consider putting down a garbage disposal: "Water and crumbs."

Maybe that warning should be on the Top Ramen or Rapid Ramen packaging — under the headline "Listen Up, Stupid."

What? Another business for Michael Broughton?

It seems that if I wait just about a month after writing about him, Michael Broughton will buy or start a new business. Well, I waited and he did. He calls his newest venture Roadtrip Media, a mobile outdoor advertising venture. That's marketing lingo for a truck that heads all over the region with rotating billboards on its sides. Broughton's tag line: "We Drive Your Business."

"The price points are dependent on the length of your buy," he tells me over a quick lunch. "Generally, ads run for about $2,000 a month — but we can also do customized routes for a bit more than that." There's no website yet but you can contact Broughton by phone (916) 447-1386 or online (michael@blanketmarketinggroup.com).

Broughton appeared in my column on Aug. 20. He's the co-owner of GrubGroupie, the online daily deal site that sells discount vouchers for food and wine. He also owns or co-owns the online restaurant guide SacDine.com and Blanket Marketing Group, which programs the ads and trivia that run between features at the Esquire IMAX Theatre in downtown Sacramento.

He recalls starting his entrepreneurial life at an early age. As a student at St. Jerome Elementary School in the Bay Area city of El Cerrito, he went the cafeteria program one better. The Catholic school's lunchroom workers would randomly distribute a limited number of "Free Hot Dog" stamps to the young diners each day. Broughton went to a store and bought blank sheets of similar stamps, then, matching the typeface as closely as possible, created his own

"Free Hot Dog" stamps. He recruited some classmates to go around selling the stamps for $1 apiece. "They got to keep 50 cents and I got 50 cents of every sale," he says.

His scheme was discovered. When it was revealed that the schemer was only in second grade, "My mom didn't quite know what to do with me. She scolded me but you could tell she was pretty proud." In his school yearbook, Broughton was quoted as saying that his dream was to one day have "Donald Trump and Merv Griffin work for me."

I remind him that Griffin has, alas, gone to that great Wheel of Fortune in the sky. "Yeah, I know," he says. "That's why now I'm working exclusively on hiring Donald Trump." I expect Broughton will land him. I'll let you know in a month or so.

Don Harris and his life after Nehemiah

On Nov. 15, which happens to be both his and my birthday, Don Harris — attorney, pastor and the original entrepreneur behind the Nehemiah Corp. — will give a breakfast talk in Sacramento's River District entitled, "Jesus, Darth Vader and the Art of Execution."

It promises to be vintage Harris, combining real-life business precepts with his faith-based belief that — well, here, let him tell you — "Jesus was not a wimp. He was unapologetic about his mission. He knew that there were times you needed to make tough, principle-based decisions about your mission. The fact that sometimes you need to fire someone doesn't make you an evil person."

Today we're having breakfast at the Original Mel's on J Street. It's the, um, ungodly hour of 7:30 on a Saturday morning. Yet as Harris chats about his reemergence into public life — the business takeover, then ultimate collapse, of Nehemiah sent him into a spiral of self-evaluation, which included keeping "a low profile for a couple of years" — he's as buoyant and filled with ideas as ever. (Full disclosure: Harris was a marketing client of mine during his Nehemiah years and though we share a birthday, I was already 14 when he was born. Please don't do the math as you read on.)

A former senior associate at the late, lamented law firm of McDonough, Holland & Allen, Harris left there long before it imploded to run Nehemiah, a Sacramento-based nonprofit that helps low and middle-income families buy homes. At the time it offered a down-payment assistance program in which home sellers helped buyers pay their closing costs by giving them a portion of the proceeds when the sale closed. The idea was to help the country's so-called "working poor" become homeowners.

For a few years in the early 2000s, Harris and the program flew close to the sun. He guested on the Today Show, won almost as much name recognition for himself as for the Nehemiah program, rubbed elbows with Oprah Winfrey and even had some serious real estate dealings with movie star Will Smith (which got Harris and his business partners invited to dinner at Smith's 80,000-sq.-ft. home in Calabasas).

But Nehemiah never sat well with the U.S. Dept. of Housing and Urban Development's then-director, now New York Gov. Andrew Cuomo. HUD didn't like the whole idea of a "gift" program — and, to be sure, Harris's concept was adapted and abused by others around the country. As lawsuits and counter-suits were filed, there was what Harris acknowledges, with amusing understatement, "some turmoil" among his community board of directors and top management. When the smoke cleared, Harris was out and a new management company was in. Today, the down-payment assistance program is no more.

The son of a Baptist pastor, Harris now divided his time between the ministry and new business ventures, including the Franklin Tanner Group, a consultancy for nonprofits. But that "turmoil" and its fallout put too much pressure on his marriage. In his early 40s he found himself divorced and occasionally demonized by business competitors. "You get to the point where you either accept the fact you're imperfect and move on from there or just give up," he says.

He didn't give up.

Monday: The second coming of Don Harris.

Oct. 29, 2012

Don Harris is a senior partner of the HMS Law Group LLP, which is housed in the upscale 455 Capitol Mall. He's also the leader of Safehaven Ministries of Sacramento, whose offices are at 1400 North C Street, in the thick of the city's homeless quarter. This is where Harris hosts business/faith breakfasts every third Thursday of the month (as I mentioned Friday, Nov. 15's topic will be "Jesus, Darth Vader and the Art of Execution").

It's also where Harris, who'll turn 48 that day, wants to kick-start a new solution to Sacramento's seemingly unsolvable homeless dilemma. He wants to create a social services district within the River District, where Loaves & Fishes — which feeds the hungry and shelters the homeless — is located, much to the consternation of neighboring business owners who believe their properties are trashed and devalued because of their proximity to various charitable venues.

Under Harris's plan — I should add that he's a respected land-use attorney whose mentors have included legendary local lawyer Joe Coomes, now of counsel to Best Best & Krieger — the social services district "would allow only one magnet provider, like Loaves & Fishes, that could provide food and shelter. Other businesses that located here would need to provide a mitigating impact on the area or offer transitional services to help people out of homelessness." Safehaven Ministries, his relatively new creation, offers outreach programs for the homeless by trying to engage businesspeople in charitable acts — "like providing a debit card to a hungry person so he or she can get a meal."

Harris says that of the three primary categories of homeless people — those who are this way voluntarily, those who are involuntarily (due to economic strife, for example) and those whom he calls "non-volitional" (the mentally ill) — Safehaven's primary population will be the involuntary homeless. He's also starting HERS, a homeless shelter exclusively for women.

Despite having dropped out of his "political connectedness" when he was forced out of Nehemiah, the affordable housing program he founded, Harris never really went underground. He's friends with Kevin Johnson, whom he helped set up the infrastructure for his various Oak Park nonprofits in Johnson's pre-mayor days. They rarely get together these days, Harris says, but it "owes more to scheduling than anything else. Let me put it this way: We'd work together in a heartbeat. But it would take a pretty large disturbance in the force of the universe to cause us to suit up together again at the same time."

These days, Harris has a new wife, son (his daughter from his first marriage is currently living in Southern California) and stepchildren. He's brimming with ideas and while his firm, the HMS Law Group, covers a wide range of specialties (real estate, estate planning, trust administration, construction, intellectual property), he wants to devote his own lawyering to serving nonprofits. I ask if this is a deliberate step back from his high-flying, high-paying days at the late McDonough Holland & Allen and Nehemiah. He smiles. "You know, Sutter Health system is a nonprofit," he says. "So's the UC system. So's the state of California and all of its agencies." I withdraw the question, counselor.

WHAT ARE THEY THINKING?

Want fries with that Chablis?

Perhaps you caught the story early this week about how some fast-food outlets and coffeehouse franchises have started serving beer and wine along with burgers and lattes.

Questions:

- Is the Happy Meal about to become the Entirely Too Happy Meal?
- Are baristas about to be called bartendas?
- Will ordering a double no longer mean an extra shot of espresso? And what about that measurement, anyway—a shot? I think Starbucks founder Howard Schultz had a lot of forethought when he dreamed up the idea of a $5 cup of coffee. "When we add booze, we won't even have to reprint the portion sizes," I can hear him saying.

Well, it's going to be disconcerting, at least for a while, to hear a voice repeating my order over the drive-through speaker: "Yessir, that's a Jumbo Jack with onion rings. Ya want Merlot with that?"

Because it's not yet clear if serving beer and wine along with McNuggets and biscotti will catch on, the companies say they're "experimenting." Who are they kidding? You only use the "e" word when you're telling your kids, grandkids or potential voters what you were doing with that marijuana cigarette in your college days.

Oct. 5, 2011

Whom do you trust: the bank or a con man?

So let me see if I understand this: To make ends meet, Bank of America is not only laying off thousands of its employees but also plans to charge us $5 for the privilege of using a debit card, tied to our own checking accounts, which is considerably riskier than using a credit card in the first place.

I learned that last part from Frank Abagnale, the author and subject of the book "Catch Me If You Can," which Steven Spielberg turned into a wonderful film of the same name. Abagnale — (pronounced AAH-bag-nail, even though you want to make it very Italian and say ah-bog-NAH-lay) — was a con man in his youth. He specialized in forging checks and being a multi-purpose imposter: doctor, lawyer, airline pilot.

As he told a crowd at the Sacramento Community Center Theater last year, if someone uses your debit card—illegally; your children in college don't count — the burdens of proof and repayment falls to you. Your money has already been stolen.

Whereas, if someone steals your credit card and uses it, you can simply refute the charge, refuse to pay and request an investigation. You'll be out nothing but some time.

I've been the victim of identity theft a few times but only once related to my debit card from Bank of America (suggested new motto: "Too Big To Fail or Manage Our Budget"). I'd be happy to admit it was my own fault — I had dumbly left the card sitting in the ATM after making a deposit — but wasn't it really the fault of the guy who took

82

the card and used it to buy a security guard jumpsuit in Fresno (I wish I were joking)?

To be fair, it wasn't very hard for me to convince the B of A's fraud unit that (a) I wasn't in Fresno that afternoon — and, in fact, try never to go there; and (b) I don't have any need for a security guard jumpsuit — unless my wife and I plan to play "Freeze, Perp!" one evening. (The fraud investigator said both editorial comments weren't germane to our discussion but allowed that he might call me back to ask more about "Freeze, Perp!")

Each time someone got hold of my VISA credit card numbers, also from B of A, the fraud unit was on the case even before I was. For example, based on my usual shopping and traveling patterns, they suspected I hadn't bought 16 DVDs of Showgirls in a Philadelphia Blockbuster store or booked three first-class airline tickets from Burbank to Hanoi.

Since I try to never buy anything with my debit card, I certainly won't start when my bank starts charging me $5 per month. And by the way: Shouldn't the makers of the debit-card machines at checkout lines consider rephrasing the instruction, "Please swipe card?" It somehow seems counterintuitive—though I may appropriate it for my next session of "Freeze, Perp!"

The down-side of exercise

E xercising on a treadmill somewhat religiously for the past year has produced a debatable added value. For the first time since I was a kid in New York City on a schools-closed snow day, I watch 30-45 minutes of daytime television a few times a week.

Snobbery has had nothing to do with my aversion to daytime TV — though I'll admit that when I was young and restless the last thing I wanted to do was watch a show revolving around characters who allegedly were. They were young, all right, but the reason they were restless was because they never seemed to get any sleep when they went to bed.

When I was an assistant director of the UC Davis Medical Center in the early 1980s, watching "General Hospital" during a coffee break held little charm for me, especially if it was realistically presented. The daily soaps rarely are, of course, though they occasionally manage to capture the mundane patter of the workplace. The one thing they never do is have a character say, "OK, for a Tuesday!" This is the screamingly witty retort to "How're you doing?" — and, as you know, a staple of mundane office patter.

All of which brings me to a staggeringly lengthy commercial I saw this holiday season for something called. I think, the LazyDay suit (I haven't been able to find it online, sorry to say): a Dr. Denton-ish full-body, zipped-velour package into which you climb and remain cozy for the rest of winter. According to the ad, you can watch TV in it or read about what's going to be on TV. You can make your favorite TV-watching snack and then go consume it while watching TV. You can also look like you weigh 350 pounds — which you very well might if you emulate the activity level of the actors in the commercial. They seem so lethargic that after they eat their pizza while watching TV, you assume they're going to just take it easy for the rest of the year.

Watching the actors waddle between kitchen and den, I got into such a giggle fit that I literally almost fell off the treadmill at Sutter Lawn Swim & Tennis Club. I was going only four miles per hour at the time but at a steep enough ascent that I'd have slid off backwards and landed on legendary artist Wayne Thiebaud, who's in his early 90s and was stretching before playing tennis with my neighbor Burnett Miller, who's in his late 80s. There must be something in the water at this club. I've never seen anyone there in a LazyDay suit.

The Santa Clara 49ers?

According to some estimates I recently compiled — in a downtown Sacramento bar, but still — it may cost a San Francisco 49ers fan as much as $80,000 per year for a good seat when the team's new $1 billion stadium opens in Santa Clara in two years. At that rate, buying a beer will require a co-signer.

As you might have read, heard or seen, a week ago tonight the Santa Clara City Council approved contracts to build the 68,500-seat arena next to Great America, the theme-less theme park. According to a story in the San Jose Business Journal, construction "is expected to begin in July, about six months ahead of the original plan."

I wonder if Santa Clara's council members would consider filling in for Sacramento's, just for one meeting. They might emerge, after only two hours of deliberation, with solid plans to: (a) develop our riverfront, Capitol Mall and K Street; (b) jump-start high-speed rail; (c) put a strong-mayor initiative on the ballot; and (d) send the Maloofs (but not the Kings) back to Nevada. My view, to paraphrase a familiar tag line, is that if the Maloofs are what's happening in Vegas, they can stay in Vegas.

I realize that expecting your average football fan to shell out $80,000 for a good seat might be unrealistic. For that price, the seat had better include not only a built-in Swedish massage but also a Swedish masseur. And a vodka dispenser, George Foreman grill, private chef and trip to Maracaibo with Dr. Oz.

On the other hand, I've come to realize that 49er fans are not "average" in any way, shape or format. I can envision 60 of them chipping in roughly $1,333 each to buy a single

seat, each one getting a few moments in it per game —
something, I'll grant you, that could be accomplished only
by smuggling several of them into a game under the largest
person's raincoat. If the raincoat contains the team's logo, I
think even skeptical guards might look the other way when
they notice that this particular customer has 14 feet.

What's bothering me about all of this, besides my not
having $80,000 handy (I changed suits earlier today),
is that I've yet to hear anyone talk about renaming the
team to reflect its new location. If Santa Clara officials,
businesspeople and fans aren't petitioning the NFL about
this — after a multi-year effort to attract the 'Niners to the
Silicon Valley — there can be only one explanation: They're
just plain pooped from driving back and forth to the Bay
Area to plead, cajole and bribe the team's owners to move.

I just hope they didn't leave their heart in San Francisco.

Not a matter of free speech

Before I chat briefly about the Stolen Valor Act of 2005 — which was signed into law a year later and is now being debated by the U.S. Supreme Court, largely the question of whether lying about your armed-services record should be protected as freedom of speech — I should first come clean about my own military exploits. I was part of the 1969 draft lottery. My birth date, Nov. 15, came up Number 131 — which, everyone said at the time, pretty much guaranteed I'd be inducted, since I'd also dropped my student deferment and was now classified 1-A. But I wasn't drafted. To everyone's surprise, they capped the draft that year at 125. As you can imagine, my lucky number became six that day.

I'd have gone into the U.S. Army if drafted but I'd be lying if I said I didn't prefer the hand I was dealt, which was essentially a lifetime parole. If you'll recall, once you survived the lottery, you were classified 1-H, which meant that for the rest of my young life, women, children and possibly multi-lingual otters would be called up before I was tapped.

To this day, I carry around some survivor guilt, and not just about having lost some classmates to the Vietnam War. For some reason, I also outlived my wife of nearly 29 years and an ex-wife of many years before that, both of who were visibly healthier and certainly saner about taking care of themselves than I.

Maybe it's this amplified sense of survivor guilt that makes me fly off the handle when I read about or find that I know people who lie about their military backgrounds. Granted, they don't really harm anyone by saying they served, saw combat and/or won awards when they didn't do anything of the sort. And I can't help but find it ironic that the act was signed into law by former Pres. George W. Bush, whose own military career, as shakily documented, perhaps proves you can go farther in life writing fiction than previously suspected.

But. To lie about wartime exploits you've never had or awards you never won — when very brave and frightened men and women risked and often made the ultimate sacrifice for the likes of all of us — strikes me as highly punishable, maybe even biblically so (I'm envisioning foreheads branded with the letter "L" for liar). This isn't a free-speech issue. No one has the inalienable right in this country to defraud the living and, by extension, defame the dead. That, my friend, is strictly un-American.

Your table is waiting

A number of restaurateurs, principally in New York City, are starting to charge people for making dinner reservations and then not showing up. According to recent reports, the no-show rate in The Big Apple has hit a paralyzing 20 percent.

In marketing about a dozen Sacramento area restaurants over the years, I learned that a customer who fails to appear is almost as frustrating for owners as having to throw out 17 pounds of duck because no one was in the mood to order that evening's special (Donald l'Orange being one of my faves). It's costly, too. In one report, a limited-seating restaurant held a table of eight for a group that went missing. Result: a shortfall of $8,000 in one night (calculated at a rate of $500 per customer; and yes, you're correct, the restaurant in question was not Applebee's).

By charging truant customers, New York restaurant owners are following a business model used by some dentists, accountants and physicians. Of course, what this latter group fails to take into account is what our time is worth if we show up as scheduled and then have to wait as much as an hour to be seen.

That's not the case with most restaurants, though I'm sure we've all had the experience of making a reservation, showing up on time and still having to wait a half-hour or more — usually in the bar, the actual profit center for many restaurants — to be seated. I usually don't get too worked up about this since no restaurant manager or efficiency expert can ever know precisely how long it will take to turn over a table (that's a figurative expression; if I were being literal, I'd be talking about a completely different type of establishment, probably one with a biker, cowboy or legislator clientele). They can make reasonable estimates but unless they're willing to approach a table of well-fed-and-marinated guests and suggest it may be time to leave and go night-night, chances are they'll be stuck with the lingerers.

I've been one of those, on many occasions. Something about the conversation, if it's flowing, and the wine, ditto, creates a sort of etiquette inertia. I see those people out there waiting for a table but I figure: Hey, I waited for this table — and to take it back, you'll have to pry it from my cold, dead hands.

Oh, wait. That was what the late Charlton Heston said about his rifle. Without reservations, I might add. And why is he late?

How to fashionably pack heat

There could be a new answer to that age-old vulgar inquiry that starts, "Is that a gun in your pocket or ... ?" That answer could be, "Yes." The New York Times reported last week that men's fashion designers are now adding hidden pockets and stretch waistbands in which to store flashlights or, more to the point, concealed weapons.

As one fellow explained, "Most of the clothes I used in the past to hide my sidearm looked pretty sloppy and had my girlfriend complaining about my looks." Then he added his endorsement of the new designs: "I'm not James Bond or nothing, but these look pretty nice." All of this prompts a few questions:

- Are we sure that the referenced girlfriend was concerned only about our fashion philosopher's "looks"? How about the fact that she's going out with someone who's armed and dangerous — someone who, if given the wrong milk percentage in his coffee drink, might be inclined to open fire on a barista?
- When the fellow said, "I'm not James Bond or nothing," what made us fairly certain that he, in fact, was not James Bond? Was it his appealing modesty or his grasp of grammar?
- What were some of the clothes our style specialist wore "in the past" to, as he indicates, hide his sidearm? What made those outfits inadequate to the task? Were they Speedos? If so, I can sympathize. Every time I head to the beach or a pool, I find it aggravating to have to wrap my Uzi in a festive towel and plop it into my wicker carryall. Why? Because

when I need to retrieve it, usually to amuse the lifeguard by picking off buoys, it always smells like potato salad.

- If your weapon is effectively concealed, how can it serve as a proper deterrent when you find yourself, say, haggling with your cleaner over whether your suit really was Martinized? What leverage will you have when you negotiate your hotel room rate if the clerk can't see a Glock "safe-action" pistol peeking out from behind your lapel?

These are the challenges that keep me up at night. Then again, maybe it's the rifle in my pajamas.

Jan. 2, 2013

Dating by the numbers

Welcome to 2013 and the brave new world of credit-score dating! According to a story in the New York Times the other day, people of all possible genders are now displaying their credit scores on first dates to indicate their suitability as partners. (Shall I compare thee to a summary report?)

I suppose this is a welcome change from sharing each other's medical records, at least from the standpoint of awkward silences. I was so naïve after I was widowed in 2007 that when a woman asked me if I'd recently been tested, I said I hadn't been a student for decades. It was our first and only date.

A credit score, as you probably know, is a rather complicated though ultimately straightforward way of determining your fiscal reliability. Banks use it — but so do landlords, insurance firms and those nice people who sold you your iPhone or 'droid. It assesses your record of paying bills on time but also guesses whether extending you some credit or lending you some dough will prove profitable.

When credit scoring is done to ascertain whether someone is worth dating, it strikes me as the cyber iteration of a dowry — though in the cases I've read about, it's generally mutual, which is a welcome change. Traditionally, it was only the father of the bride who offered a dowry to the father of the groom (or to the groom himself). The dowry could consist of money, arable land or fertile yaks. But essentially, it was a bribe: the father was paying someone to take his daughter off his hands.

I don't think money is exchanged with credit-score dating. Instead, the two people are giving each other

94

figurative promissory notes. Or even better, their RFQ (request for qualifications) before they draft up a prenuptial agreement. The message is this: You should consider marrying me because I don't bring any debt load to our potential merger.

For me, credit-score dating is probably a good thing. As I've mentioned before, the only way I'm ever going to pay off my VISA bill is if reincarnation works. I want a potential partner to know that, even if it clouds my chances of her father giving me some fertile yaks.

Wait! Tobacco is dangerous?

If you own a retail business, I demand an apology. You should have told me that the tobacco industry might not have been entirely forthright on the dangers of smoking. Unless you had told me, how would I ever have known?

If you don't post an apology immediately, I plan to fall to the ground and pound my little fists into pulps. Yes, that's how miffed I am.

But can you blame me? The Associated Press reported last week that a federal judge in Virginia will issue an opinion any second now on whether retailers should be required to put up large signs apologizing for creating "tobacco-friendly environments containing enticing displays, competitive prices and visible point-of-sale advertising." The words are those of U.S. District Judge Gladys Kessler — who, I'm going to go out on a limb and assume, is a non-smoker.

I just don't think the judge is going far enough.

I believe that clothing stores should apologize for not warning us that vertical stripes aren't flattering unless we're whippet thin. Auto dealers should say they're sorry for not giving us a heads-up that our cars will lose resale value as they age (the cars, not the dealers).

Furniture stores really ought to have kept us from carpeting our homes in wall-to-wall beige if we had pets, children or a fondness for Cabernet. Airlines that flew us across the country or around the planet should have revealed that there's a condition called "jet lag" that may have affected us once we reached our destination.

What are they thinking?

Shouldn't beauty-supply stores apologize for the fact that their products didn't actually make us beautiful, retard the aging process or permanently erase our liver spots?

Does the foregoing have you scratching your head? Maybe it's because the makers of your shampoo owe you a great big mea culpa for not making it clear that dandruff can be a chronic condition. Just like needless judicial decisions.

An unseemly recognition

According to a sign that greets you as you enter East Lawn Memorial Park, the place where my wife Jane and thousands of other people are interred has just been named "American Cemetery of the Year."

It must have been quite an awards ceremony. I can only imagine the categories (Best Supporting Bier, Best Inscription Written Directly for the Marker).

And the trade ads as the big day drew near ("For Your Consideration: East Lawn. People Are Dying to Get in Here").

And how the also-rans must have felt ("Well, it was an honor just to be nominated — which is more than you can say for Ben Affleck").

I realize I'm being tasteless. But so is East Lawn.

I know that every business needs to promote itself in a competitive marketplace. And if you've ever handled the funeral arrangements for a loved one, you know that the "up-sell" is alive and well at mortuaries, mausoleums and cemeteries. Why else would there be full-color catalogues to page through, featuring a wide range of prices on coffins and cremation urns, while you're sitting and trying to not implode with grief or explode with anger?

But aren't there some companies and industries that ought to know better than to put up signs that would be more appropriate on Sunset Boulevard ("The Number One Comedy In America!")? Does everything we do need to be motivated by the prospect of winning an award for it?

I Googled the presenter of the American Cemetery Excellence award — yes, the coveted ACE — and you can, too. On it I found the obligatory "Call For Entries" and this write-up: "If you think your team should be recognized for maintaining a great cemetery that's succeeding in tough economic times, then we want to hear from you. It doesn't matter if you are owned by a corporation, a municipality or by an independent entity; we are seeking entries from top-performing cemeteries to recognize your accomplishments."

But hey, there are criteria: "While this is an award recognizing the overall cemetery, we ask for finalists to be prepared to make a cemetery staff member available to be interviewed." Why not a satisfied customer?

OK, that's silly. But why not ask for pre-death testimonials? "I have a choice to be buried in any number of graveyards. But I'm choosing East Lawn Memorial Park. Why? Because it won the ACE award. And that's good enough for me!"

Where do we go from here? Should we "like" East Lawn on Facebook?

Not I, pal.

CORPORATE EXECS

A dash of Estelle Saltzman

E stelle Saltzman's business partner, mentor and dear friend Jean Runyon battled and conquered a host of illnesses during the past few decades, marrying and burying a few husbands along the way. But it still surprised Saltzman when Runyon died at 82 in 2009. "I didn't really expect her to ever leave," she says.

The two met in 1972 and would gradually become partners in what's now called Runyon, Saltzman & Einhorn, which this very publication cited as the region's second highest-billing advertising agency in a recent Top 25 list. Runyon — an actress, political activist, art collector, philanthropist and well-known madcap — was "the yin to my yang," Saltzman tells me a week ago. "I was a reporter and editor and pretty serious. Jean was lively and engaging, a genuine entertainer. We met when she was doing public relations for the State Fair and hired me to do press releases. She was so funny that it took me a while to get used to being around her."

I ask how long. Saltzman smiles shyly. "About a nanosecond," she says.

"When we started working together," she says, "she was always making fun of me for being grumpy. But there was this instant rapport. I think we met at a time when we simply had room for each other in our lives."

The Runyon agency, as it's familiarly known, is heading back to thrive mode after a year in which, Saltzman says, "We just broke even. I realize that's a lot better than some other agencies and businesses did and I'm very grateful. But 2012 looks pretty darned good." The firm hired five new employees in one month: it now has a staff of 44; nearly all are full-time.

We're chatting in the agency's fourth-floor offices in the One Capitol Mall building. Dressed comfortably in a soft purple sweater and dark slacks, Saltzman looks out the window at her views of the Tower Bridge, the Sacramento River and, notably, Raley Field. "I keep a (catcher's) mitt here in my office and catch foul balls," she says, completely deadpan. As I look for, but don't find, an outside balcony that would allow her to do so, she grins impishly. "Gotcha," she says almost inaudibly.

The not-entirely-solemn Saltzman was born to Max and Bernice Goodman, a physician and homemaker, in Eureka not quite 70 years ago. She always wanted to be a reporter and began her career in high school, writing stories for the Humboldt Times. She left to attend UCLA, where she met her husband of 22 years, Mort Saltzman, now retired from the Sacramento Bee (they divorced in the 1980s). She graduated from UC Berkeley with a degree in political science.

"Jeanie was always giving money to causes and starving artists or not billing clients when she felt they were having a hard time financially. I told her we ought to put a tag line under our agency's sign: 'A Nonprofit Corporation.'" Apparently, madcap is a contagious condition.

Tomorrow: An award named for Jeanie — and a special guest appearance by Omar (Dr. Zhivago) Sharif.

Jan. 6, 2012

"It occurred to me at some point that we had people working here at the agency who'd never met Jeanie," Estelle Saltzman says of her late business partner, mentor and pal, Jean Runyon. "Some were people we'd hired even when she was still alive. I didn't want anyone to ever forget her. And I wanted everyone to meet her, in some way."

That way was the creation of the annual Jeanie, a cash-and-gift-cards award and plaque. It goes to an employee of Runyon, Saltzman & Einhorn — the local advertising and public relations agency that currently bills about $25 million, according to the Sacramento Business Journal's Top 25 list — who best exemplifies Runyon's qualities and talents. Award-winning traits include ingenuity, graciousness, diplomacy, effectiveness, persistence and, of course, success.

This year, Saltzman and her partners — Jane Einhorn, Scott Rose, Chris Holbein and Paul McClure — selected one of the firm's art directors, Greg Ries, as the Jeanie winner. He says the award left him "verklempt" — which the firm's website helpfully points out is Yiddish for "gob-smacked." (For those of you for whom neither word is familiar, let me take a stab at it: It also means "kerfuffled.")

Saltzman will be 70 in April and tells me, "I have no intention of retiring the way Jeanie did — which was not quite at all." Runyon, she says, came into the office, somewhat unpredictably, until shortly before she died at 82 in 2009. "I plan to work through 2012, then take a look at cutting back in 2013," she says.

She doesn't hesitate for a moment when asked what she'll do with her free time: Saltzman is a bridge player with a Life Master designation. "I'll get back into this," she promises her visitor — and probably herself.

Playing bridge is more glamorous than it might sound — or at least some of its players are. Saltzman recalls playing "a couple of hands" in Los Angeles some years back with no less than Omar Sharif, the liquid-eyed, dashing star of Dr. Zhivago, Funny Girl and McKenna's Gold (an incredibly silly western that I happen to love). He told her as they played,

"Women are not to play bridge with. You can dance with them and marry them. But you can't play bridge with them."

Saltzman won't say, but my hope is that she ended up beating his dashing pants off.

Sacramento Hyatt chief
Scott VandenBerg

L ate last week I popped over to the Hyatt Regency Sacramento, which threw itself a reception to celebrate the $3 million renovation of its lobby. This was the second phase of a multimillion-dollar upgrade the hotel started in 2009, which included renovation of its 500-plus guest rooms — including the 12th floor suite that former Gov. Arnold Schwarzenegger rarely called home, media reports to the contrary notwithstanding. (He flew home to Southern California most nights on a private jet, according to a reliable source: him.)

I chatted briefly with Scott VandenBerg, the relatively new general manager — I say "relatively" because even though he's been at this Hyatt only since last year, he's been with the Hyatt Hotels Corporation for 32 years. This is the 17th hotel he's opened.

"It's always like giving birth," he says. Having interviewed or profiled three of VandenBerg's predecessors at the Sacramento Hyatt over the years, I knew that the hotel's home office likes to place GMs at its inns for a minimum, and usually a maximum, five-year stint. He replaced Ulrich Samietz as GM here; Samietz is now in Vancouver. Jerry Westenhaver, another former Hyatt GM in Sacramento, is now in Maui.

"Yes, I've been all over," VandenBerg says, naming some of his past job sites: San Francisco, San Diego, Los Angeles, Atlanta, Maui, Vancouver, Canada, and several cities in Florida. The globe-girding manager currently lives in Greenhaven with his wife Rachael, who's also in the hotel business — and job hunting. "The Hyatt has rules about couples working in the same hotel," VandenBerg says.

The new-and-improved lobby is elegant and uncluttered. My favorite feature is the rethinking of Hyatt's check-in desk, which now allows clerks to step around and chat with you rather than have them stand behind A Very Important Counter which featured all the warmth of a bank, Togos or, best yet, an urgent-care facility. The Hyatt seems to understand, more than many hotels, that it's in the hospitality, not hospital, business.

Shannon Deary-Bell
takes golf seriously

Shannon Deary-Bell says she didn't plan to go into the family business. Now, at 45, she's the president and chief executive officer of Nor-Cal Beverage Co. Inc., the national beer, water and juice distributor based in West Sacramento with another major distribution plant in Anaheim. "It just kind of evolved," she says over a hamburger salad at Lucca.

She had played golf for USC's team then worked in membership sales for the tony La Cañada Flintridge Country Club in Los Angeles County. "I never had this overwhelming desire to join the company," she says. Then one day her father, company president Don Deary, called her. "Ever since his brother (Grant Deary) had died in 1999, he'd started thinking about the subject of succession. He said, 'Come on up here and just give it a try.' So I did, but I didn't like it at first."

She asked her father if she could work in the company's Stockton branch, which was a distribution center and Nor-Cal's only Teamster connection. "We broke the union five years after I got there," she says. Today, the company's 576 full-time employees have their own, in-house union. "Our people run into and talk to members of other unions all the time," Deary-Bell says, "so it's not as if they don't know what industry standards are for pay and benefits. They certainly know how to negotiate for themselves."

Eventually, Deary-Bell worked her way up into the company's corporate offices as its marketing director. After a few years, she found herself being interviewed, as were other family members, for the job she now holds. "When I got the job, I started finding out how few women CEOs there are in this industry," she says.

Nor-Cal bubbled to life 75 years ago. Deary-Bell's grandfather, Roy Deary, founded the company; its first job was bottling cases of Hire's Root Beer. It would eventually bottle more than 25,000 cases of soft drinks a day. But five years ago, Nor-Cal sold its bottling franchise.

"We couldn't compete globally with companies like Coca-Cola," Deary-Bell says. So Nor-Cal's management team "hunkered down" and changed its focus to distributing beer, working for Anheuser-Busch, the nation's largest brewery (its market share of beer sales to United States retailers is nearly 50 percent, according to various industry sources). It also got into serious R&D, creating its own line of energy drinks, Go Girl, and saw its co-packing activity — of tea, water and juice drinks — grow to become the largest independent operation of its kind in the West.

Deary-Bell is an avid golfer. Her husband, Brad Bell, is a golf course designer (he's also the son of one of this region's most respected attorneys, now retired: Bob Bell). She says that one of her company's informal initiation rites for new hires is playing a round of golf with her. "When you play 18 holes with somebody, you learn a lot about them — about their integrity, their honesty, their intellect," she says.

Deary-Bell asks me what my own handicap is, and I answer, "Golf." "Then I guess you won't be coming to work for us," she says with a smile.

Meet Steve Fleming

Steve Fleming, the president and CEO of River City Bank, is telling me over lunch that the bank's new strategic partnership with Genovese Burford & Brothers, one of the largest financial planning firms in the region, was "almost a no-brainer. It was the right fit from a corporate culture standpoint. We have the same target market. We're both locally owned, make decisions quickly, aren't bureaucracies and believe in high-touch service."

As the Business Journal has reported, RCB in June bought a 20 percent ownership stake in Burford, which is celebrating its first quarter-century this year.

"We didn't want the bank to buy a controlling interest because we didn't want to start imposing our style on Burford," Fleming says over a Caesar salad in the grill room at downtown's Sutter Club. "Their customers are still their customers, and ours are still ours, but we're referring people back and forth."

The Burford firm has about $1.3 billion in "assets under advisement" (an industry term that simply means the dough isn't in its own piggy bank). Its offices will remain in the Point West area near Cal Expo.

River City Bank, which was founded in 1973, also boasts assets of more than $1 billion. While it has 13 branches in four counties, "We couldn't offer the wealth management and retirement services that GBB does," Fleming says. "We'd refer our customers to firms that we trusted. Eventually, it was clear that the one we referred (to) most often was Burford."

While his marketing people and his own face-time sensibility have made Fleming somewhat ubiquitous for a banker, it's still surprising how gentle, funny and unprepossessing he is. Tall, bespectacled and rail-thin, he looks more like the not-overly-happy farmer in Grant Wood's "American Gothic" than the tenacious athlete and competitive businessman he is.

How tenacious? Last December he clocked up a 3:32 time for running the California International Marathon, a feat that qualifies him to run in the Boston version of the 26.2-mile race this coming spring.

"My age was actually an asset," he says. "The Boston Marathon puts you in age groups when they qualify you — but it's the age you'll be when you run it, not the age you might have been when you ran another race that qualified you."

To recap: Fleming was 53 when he ran the California race and earned points for his time. He's now 54. But he turns 55 on March 5; that puts him into the older-guy category for the Boston Marathon, in which he'll compete on April 15. He enters with a slight competitive edge.

"I don't know how long my lower body's going to let me do this," Fleming says. "For now, I want to finish this out with style and not be known as just a weekend runner." Or one who only keeps bankers' hours.

Nancy Fisher shows who's boss

Nancy Fisher is telling me, over coffee in her private conference room, that her first experience producing a promotional video for the senior communities she and her late husband Hank Fisher were developing, back in the late 1970s, "was a disaster. Everyone looked 110 years old in it. We showed it in our sales trailer for a maximum of two weeks. Every senior who saw it said, 'I don't want to live with all of those old people' — even if they were the same age or even older than the people in the video."

Fisher is the president and CEO of Hank Fisher Properties, a role she stepped into when her husband, a CPA and entrepreneur, died of a brain tumor in 2006. She had been her husband's go-to person for interior design but "wasn't that involved in the business."

Nevertheless, "I always put in my two cents' worth. Like I'd see the bathrooms in our properties had orange shower curtains and blue polka-dot bathmats and I'd say, 'This simply won't do!'" She says her husband encouraged her to make other changes. "I told him, 'Give me a budget.' And he just laughed and said, 'Oh, just do what you have to do.'" She grins and sips her coffee. "So I did."

Playful, stylishly coiffed and dressed, Fisher energetically takes me on a tour of River's Edge, the elegantly appointed retirement development nestled behind the Campus Commons golf course on Feature Drive. "I like my places to look like the Ritz Carlton," she says, pointing out the tasteful paintings and prints, richly patterned carpeting and neutral walls. When I tell her I once was married in the San Francisco Ritz Carlton, she smiles, perhaps indulgently, and says, "No, I mean the one at Half Moon Bay." (I wait in vain for her to punctuate this with, "Dahhhling.")

I ask Fisher if, when she lost her husband and decided to assume leadership of the company's now five full-service senior communities and assorted apartment developments, there was resentment among managers who might have thought they'd be Hank's professional successors. "Not that I ever heard," she says. Pressing the issue, I ask if anyone ever tells her: "Well, Hank would have done it this way."

Huge grin. "Oh, all the time," she says, breaking into a laugh. Then she repeats it with even more merriment. "All the time!"

The Fishers were married 48 years. Their daughter, Wendy, who lives in the Northwest, has two little girls. I ask Fisher if she feels she's grown into the role she says she never foresaw taking on.

"I do," she says swiftly, "but I can tell you that I wish I knew six years ago what I know now."

Examples? "We really didn't have much competition when we started out," she says. "To go back to what I said a moment ago, when people tell me that Hank would have done something differently than I do, they forget that times changed and the economy changed. To be honest, I think Hank Fisher would have made a lot of the decisions I've made. He was a sharp businessman and he recognized when it was time to shift his thinking."

I guess that's why they stopped showing that video with the old-looking people.

John Frisch on real estate

John Frisch tells me over lunch that he learned he didn't want to be a farmer during the years he was one, growing plums and almonds in Clovis. The circumstances make his decision understandable. When his father began to suffer a series of heart attacks, Frisch took over running the family farm. He was 12 years old.

Today, a few weeks from his 61st birthday, Frisch is regional marketing director of the Sacramento and Roseville offices of the impossibly long-named Cornish & Carey Commercial Network Knight Frank. He also chairs the Sacramento Metro Chamber of Commerce and spends more time on more boards than Greg Louganis.

We're lunching at Mulvaney's Building & Loan in midtown, a venue Frisch has chosen, he says with a huge grin, "because you always mention where you interview people and I really like this place and the owners." (He's referring to Patrick and Bobbin Mulvaney.) It's a jovial remark but also typifies the 6-foot-4 Frisch's literal and figurative largesse.

Another example: Since a downtown parking meter had just rejected my credit card, I tell Frisch there may be an embarrassing conclusion to the meal I'm allegedly treating him to when the check arrives. He just laughs and shakes his head. "Oh, I think I can handle it," he says. (My card ends up going through Mulvaney's machine just fine, however. Damn.)

I ask Frisch if his 20-plus years with Cornish & Carey, which were preceded by a very successful 10-year stint with CB Richard Ellis, helped him formulate any sort of general theories about commercial real estate investing. He gives me a quick answer then pauses and waves one of his cinderblock-sized hands in front of me. "No, forget I said all that," he says. "Here's what I've learned. Sometimes people forget that you make money in commercial real estate when you buy, not when you sell. If you own a good piece of real estate and you're not over-leveraged, it's almost impossible to lose money."

On the other hand, he goes on, "People got into the mentality some years ago that you simply couldn't overpay for real estate. After all, this is California." He smiles a bit ruefully, then repeats, this time with evident irony, "I mean, it's California! What could possibly go wrong?"

Tomorrow: Frisch shares some secrets of his firm's (and his) success.

Nov. 13, 2012

"I have no hobbies," John Frisch says in responding, modestly and humorously, to a question about what one might call — admiringly — his compulsive philanthropy.

He's won the Trainor Fairbrook Humanitarian of the Year, which is presented to real estate professionals who remember they're also part of the community they market, four times. Five years ago the Salvation Army honored him with a similar award at a luncheon that attracted around 1,300 businesspeople and politicos and, more to the point, netted $300,000 for the charity. "I was very proud of that," Frisch says, "since as a faith-based charity, the Salvation Army can't apply for most of the grants out there." Going himself one better, Frisch recently chaired a $7.4 million capital campaign for the group.

Speaking of his industry, Frisch says, "It's getting harder to find new college graduates who want to go into a totally commissioned business. They want job security and benefits. It's all about making money in this field but it takes more than knowledge and training, which we're happy to provide. It takes energy and heart."

Frisch says he sees the economy improving "a little" but admits that his firm had grown "overly dependent on government and the homebuilding industry," which were devastated in the recession that officially began in 2008 but had been moldering for at least two years before that. Nevertheless, Frisch's firm, Cornish & Carey — if you want to see the full, jaw-paralyzing name, please see yesterday's column — is poised to soar again in the next few years.

"One of our major clients is the State of California's General Services Agency, which is by far the largest commercial real estate tenant in the region," he says. "They lease 25 percent of all the office space in Sacramento, which amounts to 20 million square feet. It's our very own 800-pound gorilla."

Cornish & Carey (which sounds to me, I'm sorry, like a Scottish take-out restaurant) also lists among its clients Facebook and LinkedIn. Perhaps you've heard of those feisty little start-ups.

Frisch's wife of 10 years, Maggie, is a residential real estate broker with Lyon. He has two grown daughters from his previous marriage: Amy, 32, and Megan, 29. "They're smarter than I am," he deadpans.

"I have my most fun today acting as a professional cheerleader for our agents," Frisch says, explaining that he no longer does any selling. Asked if he misses it, he looks as if he's about to share a very large secret. His eyes widen, he adjusts his glasses, then smiles warmly as he exhales and slowly says, "Not. One. Bit."

Meet marketing guru Lila Wallrich

"I'm kind of like a translator," Lila Wallrich says as we yack in the very cool conference room of her very cool offices at 2020 L St. in midtown. "Clients like when I'm the one, along with the appropriate staff person, who shows up, and not just for the initial meeting. My showing up signals to them, 'Your business is important to me.'

"After all, the firm's called Wallrich," she adds, somehow making the statement sound simultaneously sincere and, because of its obviousness, ironic.

The advertising and marketing firm is the latest iteration of Wallrich Landi, which opened in 1990. A year ago November, Wallrich bought out her longtime partner, Susan Landi. She moved her staff into its current digs almost exactly a year later.

While she has the lanky physique and sparkly enthusiasm of an avid 20-year-old tackling her first real job, Wallrich, a Sacramento native, is 49. "I have all these young hipsters working for me," she says with the smile I've never seen her without in the years I've known her. She's pretty hip herself: a hybrid of creativity and technology who was figuring out social-media strategies for her clients (and taking notes on one of the first Palm Pilots in existence) before anyone even called it social media. "People are a little surprised that I can speak both design and business," she says.

Some of her clients include, have included or will include again (since almost everyone who's hired her firm rehires it) Western Health Advantage, the Sacramento Public Library, SMUD's Smart Sacramento program, Grebitus and Sons jewelers and a number of area law firms. She and I worked together briefly almost a decade ago when I suggested calling several city of Sacramento departments "SacrAmenities." Wallrich's staff carried out (and greatly improved) the branding.

Wallrich's firm does message development, creates tag lines and logos and not only conceives of and designs websites but also writes code for them. The latter is relatively rare for a marketing firm, which often turns over that task to a tech firm. "We were probably the first firm here to do all of the programming in-house," she says. "But I like giving end-to-end service." The firm has won so many awards for its marketing and other services that it cheekily piles them into a clear tower in the waiting room rather than build elaborate trophy cases.

One of Wallrich's proudest recent accomplishments sounds as though I'm kidding but I'm certainly not: her firm created "a condom-finder app" for the Center for AIDS Research, Education & Services, a local nonprofit clinic established in 1989 at the height of the HIV epidemic. "It provides the location and contact information of vendors, wherever you are, should you find yourself in need," Wallrich says.

Tomorrow: Wallrich explains why she took art classes "to annoy my parents."

Feb. 7, 2013

Lila Wallrich, the CEO and creative director of her self-named strategic marketing firm, says she took art classes in college "probably just to annoy my parents, who expected me to go into the sciences."

Her now-retired dad, John Wurschmidt, was a civil engineer for CalTrans and her mom, Lee, is a math teacher

— "and I mean one who teaches the hard stuff, like calculus, which I happen to like."

While Wallrich was born in Sacramento, her father's work took the family "as far north as the Smith River and as far south as San Diego," she tells me in her light-filled conference room at 20th and L Streets in midtown Sacramento. "I had engineering and math in my DNA," she says, which is why, combined with her communication and design skills, she remains what's called a double-threat as a marketing professional: she's equally creative and tech-oriented.

Wallrich has 19 full-time staff members. Sometimes, at the end of a grueling week, they "drag me into participating in an office super-quiz" — a trivia contest that takes no prisoners. (I've offered to have her bring me to one of these as a ringer since, as faithful readers know, no one can be more trivial than I can. Or is that petty and clumsy?) For a number of years she's been a dedicatee of Irish dancing and proudly points out that she was the member of the team that won the North American Championship of the San Francisco-based Whelan-Kennelly Academy of Irish Dance. "We won in the division for adult ladies," she says — then adds, while holding up and satirically waving two fingers at me, like a precocious kid, "Twice!"

Wallrich's husband of 26 years, Brad, is a service guy for George Gudie Heating & Air Conditioning Service, Inc., a fact I mention because he's been to my house numerous times and in all of those years I never made the connection that he and Lila were a couple. "Brad was in the restaurant management business," Wallrich says, "but we figured out early on in our marriage that one of us ought to be doing something sane."

As I prepare to leave, I ask Wallrich if she's still having fun. She drops the glowing grin for a moment and says,

Corporate execs

"What I feel about my work, and this is the God's honest truth, is that when I was 10 or 11 years old, I kind of dreamt up what I'd like to do for a living someday. I wanted to be creative and arty but I wanted to figure out how things worked. This is truly the job I imagined for myself."

I'm sure her parents weren't annoyed by her choice.

TECHNOLOGY

An early business mistake

O ne of my first and silliest moves when I became a full-time marketing/PR consultant in 1982 was to sign up with an answering service.

At the time, electronic voicemail was a pricey rarity—and I hated my answering machine, anyway, whose reel-to-reel tape was constantly folding or entangling itself, making my voice on the outgoing message sound like Kermit the frog's.

I also thought it would sound more professional—and my one-man office would somehow seem vaster—if someone besides me took my calls. It didn't turn out that way.

The service I hired wasn't equipped to answer the phone and summon me to pick it up. In other words, if the service answered, all I could do was return the call after I got the message—which I could get only by calling the service. No one there ever called me.

But there was another problem. The service's employees had — how shall I put this? — highly variable skill sets. One found the English language, specifically the part about having nouns and verbs agree, to be an ongoing challenge. Another so badly mangled the pronunciation of some of my clients' names that I ended up not returning calls because I assumed they'd been placed by telemarketers.

The situation became so frustrating that one afternoon I forwarded my calls to the service, and then used a different phone in my home office to call me. It went something like this:

"Goman Medium." (My company originally was called Goldman Media.)

"Hi," I said, "is Mr. Goldman in?"

"No."

Silence.

"Uh — do you expect him?" I asked.

"He don't ever come in. I ain't ever seen him."

"He don't? You ain't?"

"Right."

"But he will return my call, won't he?"

"Sure. I'll tell him you called."

"Good. My name's — "

But she had already hung up.

I've used voicemail ever since. As has the whole gang here at Goman Medium.

Two essential car gadgets

A ccording to a report that came out the other day, U.S. and foreign automakers may not care as much about building the safest, most fuel-efficient cars on the road as competing with each other to see which one can cram the most high-tech, glistening and unnecessary gadgetry into its products.

This isn't that new a trend. I can recall when "hydromatic" (as opposed to manual-shift) transmission cars came rolling off Detroit's assembly lines. They'd actually been around since the 1940s but weren't mass-produced until I showed up in the 1950s; it was nice of them to wait.

I remember when you could buy a "push-button" sedan so you wouldn't have to exhaust yourself, poor baby, moving the stick on your steering wheel or floor into gear. And I have fond memories of my dad's third-hand 1952 shutter-green Oldsmobile Delta 88, which featured an early version of a global positioning system: a dash-mounted, circular compass that told you the direction in which you were driving, sometimes accurately. It was just a step above what you'd use in your Conestoga to find the Oregon Trail.

In the near future, you'll be able to do everything from voting on an IPO to making waffles while hurdling down I-5 to get to the California High-Speed Rail station in downtown Coachella. Here are two additional features I'm looking forward to seeing:

- **Touch-Screen Neurotic Channel Changers.**
  What can be more fun on a lengthy trip or just a jaunt through town than having a passenger who changes radio stations with the dexterity, speed and transfixed

focus of a texter on amphetamines? Well, what if that person isn't available one day? How will you cope without the brain- and ear-jarring cacophony of rap, rock, jazz, news and commentary, not to mention traffic updates in Ukrainian, blaring at you and causing your blood pressure to achieve bold new highs? Now, by just saying, "Irritate me to death" to your rearview mirror, you'll activate a nonstop barrage of completely non-complementary sounds.

- **Voice-Activated Sign Readers.** My Midwestern in-laws, a marriage ago, had this delightful habit of reading aloud every single billboard and road sign on drives lasting a minimum of three hours. Let me repeat that: Every. Single. Damned. One. If you have or had in-laws like these, perhaps you miss them and have grown nostalgic for their incessant recitation. This amenity allows you to click a tiny switch on your steering wheel, which activates a computer voice that asks you to identify how you'd like your voice-activated sign readers to sound: Midwestern? Elderly? Noo Yawk-ish ("Hey, look, is dat a Moiduh Boiguh joint up ahead!")? Choose the pitch and style that best triggers your aggravation scale. Xanax not included.

Five brilliant ideas for Apple

Some fervent disciples of all things Apple have been posting their dissatisfaction with the company's decision to not christen its newest product with a clever or at least vaguely Zen-like name. As you know, this is the kind of pitched battle that can erupt when certain people have too much time on their hands and have run out of Skittles and Jolt Cola.

When this tempest-in-a-pizza-box broke, Phil Schiller, Apple's senior veep of worldwide marketing, told the Wall Street Journal that the company would be referring to its latest doohickey only as "the new iPad." And why? "Because we don't want to be predictable," he said.

I have a different theory. I think the R&D gang at Apple came up with the device and, in the rush of things, neglected to send a memo to the company's branding department. Therefore, I think a good name for the product would be "iForgot."

It's a shame, really. I've loved and used Apple products since 1989, which apparently made me the last kid on the block to do so. Over the years, I've suggested several new products to them in a series of unsolicited and evidently undelivered emails. Here are some of them:

- iPadMyExpenseAccount, an app for traveling executives, salespeople and elected officials on familiarization tours.
- iPed, a music player that slips onto your bare foot while you're trying on sandals.

- iStea, a summery beverage that you can swig while texting every few seconds (you need to say this one aloud).
- iStandCorrected, a dual-purpose gizmo that can be used by talk-show hosts to issue blanket apologies via a special Twitter account, and also a low-impact orthotic for sciatica sufferers.
- iDon'tHaveALife, a chat-room facilitator that brings together people who complain about product names. Skittles and Jolt Cola sold separately.

Car safety for drinkers

A new technology will soon allow your car to not only check your blood-alcohol level but also refuse to start if it doesn't approve of the results. It's called the Driver Alcohol Detection System for Safety, or DADSS — though it seems to me that if you say this acronym aloud, you'll already sound somewhat drunk.

I feel about the device the way I do, and have often expressed, about time-management seminars — namely, that if you can find the time to attend one, you don't really need to go. The DADSS comes with a similar built-in irony: If you need to check your blood-alcohol level before you drive, perhaps you should consider not driving, even before you get the results.

I'd like to suggest some other driver-safety issues and potential life-saving devices that the Alliance of Automobile Manufacturers and the National Highway Traffic Safety Administration — which sponsored development of DADSS — might want to focus on:

- TEXTECUTION. As soon as this gadget senses you're texting while driving, it will eject you through the top of your car at 100 miles an hour, whether or not you have a sunroof. In short, you'll become your own hash-mark, Tweeters! Bandages sold separately.
- TURN, TURN, TURN. This device will be able to detect that you're planning to make a turn at the next intersection but, unlike you, will switch on your turn signal before you arrive at the stoplight! It's an amazing concept, I realize, but think how many incidences of road rage will be prevented when all

of the drivers behind you — who could have shifted into another lane if they knew you were going to turn when the light flashed green — are notified of your intention.

- GARAGE HAND. Remember when the City of Sacramento economized by getting rid of its parking-lot attendants? (The savings, I'm sure, will help finance the new arena — or at least the pre-development fees the community-spirited Maloofs, otherwise known as the Brothers Catchyalater, don't feel they should have to pay. I digress.) We're reminded, from the time we enter city-owned garages, to hang onto the tickets we received at the entry gate. But most of us forget, at least on one or 74 occasions. GARAGE HAND won't let that happen anymore. This flexible device, which looks just like a small human hand, jumps off your dashboard and into your shirt or blouse pocket when you park. It then reaches up and slaps your face repeatedly until you slide the ticket into your pocket, alongside the device. Note: GARAGE HAND can also be used to discourage overly zealous dates or to revive victims of the TEXTECUTION device.

A high-tech fix for cocktail parties

T wo stories in the Wall Street Journal last week are related but neither the reporters nor most readers would readily see the connection. This is why you have me.

One story discussed techniques for zeroing in on a single conversation at a cocktail party, an event that tends to be cacophonous, at least if organized properly. The other dealt with a new generation of alarm clocks that sense when you're actually ready to climb out of bed, which is not necessarily the time you programmed as your wake-up call. It's all about when you start moving around, which the clock reads as "sleeping lightly." Why that doesn't register as "getting frisky" may be a question for its inventors when they get to the 2.0 version.

You may be asking: Why are these stories related? But since most of you have been to cocktail parties — which was my unofficial minor in college and is an area in which I've done many years of post-graduate work — perhaps you've already made the logical leap.

What we really need is a device to wake us up at cocktail parties when the conversation on which we're focusing threatens to deliver us to Dreamland.

Frankly, drifting off or away can be a problem even if you're not imbibing and even when you're not at a cocktail party. Just try listening to an insurance rep tell you why a whole-life policy is "just like a savings account," or a techie discuss your computer's operating system. Try not to slump noticeably when someone under the age of, say, 25, holds forth about the relative merits of Goyte Featuring Kimbra's version of "Somebody That I Used to Know" compared to

"We Are Young," a song by a group called (the following lowercase is correct) fun. Both songs are atop the Hot 100 chart. I bet you didn't know that.

Have you ever been at an art show, admired a piece and then made the unfortunate decision to read the Artist's Statement? The ones I write for my own work are deliberately ridiculous (but then, so are most of the art pieces I create). They're not intended to make fun of the interested observer, only of the need for the statement. This is one of my flaws, I realize. I fully support D.H. Lawrence's maxim, "Never trust the author, trust the tale." Which means, of course, that if my work isn't doing it for you, then what I meant you to get out of it is meaningless.

I bet your eyelids are growing heavy.

If my phone's so smart, why does it get lost?

Was it Mick Jagger who once sang, "Sometimes you get what you want but you lose what you've got"? And if so had he purchased an iPhone then forgot where he left it and had to purchase a replacement, as I had?

We all know the trauma of having our computers crash, our Internet server go down, or someone call us a rude name, inspiring everyone in the room to burst into sustained applause. Losing a cellphone is a little more serious, however.

I didn't always feel this way. Last year, someone broke into my car — well, I'd left it unlocked, so it was more like someone climbed into my car — and made off with my previous, decidedly outmoded cellphone. (How outmoded? The numbers were in Roman numerals.) But because I had promised to pick someone up that evening at Sacramento Unintentional Airport, I realized there might have been a sudden need to communicate ("I missed the train." "I thought you were on the plane." "I was, then on the airport train." "The airport has a train?"). So I rushed to a phone store and impulsively bought an iPhone 4.

Well, "impulsively" might not be the right adverb. As you know, the first time you venture into the brave new world of smart-phones, you're in the store for at least 140 minutes, listening to instructions on how to do things you know you'll never need or even want to do with your new gadget.

Accordingly, when I lost my iPhone 4 this week, I mounted a serious search for it, looking in every room

135

in my house, every inch of my car and every shelf in my refrigerator. This last locale is not, unfortunately, a joke. In my decades with the Dept. of Earth, I've found sets of keys, pairs of eyeglasses and the opening chapter of my autobiography there.

I ultimately realized there was no option but to replace the damn thing. I budgeted two hours, $500 and one myocardial infarction. Yet at the AT&T Store in University Village, a very efficient and gracious young woman named Monica had me in and out of the store, with a brand new iPhone 4S, in about 25 minutes, most of which were taken up by my asking her to put the phone in the protective cover for me, connect me to the Internet and why she thought a man of my age would leave his keys in the refrigerator.

OFFICIALS, LAWYERS AND POLITICOS (OH, MY!)

Sept. 22, 2011

My pal Anthony Kennedy

U.S. Supreme Court Justice Anthony Kennedy was in town this past weekend to help dedicate the remodeled Legal Studies Center (which I believe was formerly known as the law liberry) at the Pacific McGeorge School of Law.

Kennedy, a local boy who made verrrrry good, is the longest serving faculty member at McGeorge and a highly respected scholar. But I like him because he's also pretty funny. Looking around the contemporary, airy, two-story, building, he told the crowd of judges, lawyers, law students and, in my case, tag-along spouses, that inviting him to speak was "the subtlest way to remind me I have an overdue book."

At a reception prior to the ribbon cutting, I had a chance to remind Kennedy that he and I had a brief print exchange when he was confirmed for the Supreme Court in 1988. At the time, everyone in town was, understandably, claiming to have known "Tony" for decades. Many had. Many hadn't.

So I wrote, in my then-column for the Sacramento Business Journal, that I wanted to state for the record that I not only didn't know Justice Kennedy but also that I'd never met much less seen him in person. He wrote me this note on McGeorge letterhead, which I somehow lost during two or three moves but have committed to memory: "Dear Ed: I've never met you, either! —Tony."

139

My interview with Gov. Rick Perry

I felt a little sad for soon-to-be-former Republican presidential hopeful Rick Perry when, as they say in show business, he went up on his lines at a debate last week.

As you can guess, "went up" means plumb forgot what he was supposed to say. Poor Gov. Perry couldn't remember the name of one of the federal departments he plans to annihilate if he were to move into the White House in 2013.

I'm no fan of Perry's but I do know something about public speaking, having done a lot of it, coached people on how to do it and screwed up many times while doing it.

The worst speaking experience I ever had, however, which wasn't really my fault, occurred 21 years ago. I was asked to give a funny talk at the Christian Brothers High School reunion. I was recovering from pneumonia so didn't have a great deal of vocal strength but was assured by Terry Flynn, who'd invited me, that there'd be a microphone.

There was indeed. There was also a great-hall full of guys ranging in chronological age from perhaps 18 to 85, and behaving, that night, like 3- to 4-year-olds on fructose corn syrup highs. I vaguely recall a food fight. People were shouting at each other across the cavernous room. Nobody heard me being introduced, much less what I had to say.

About a minute into it, I turned to Flynn and asked if I'd get paid even if I stopped speaking right now. He nodded a bit morosely. So I stopped, thanked the crowd, grabbed the check and was about to drive home when all of a sudden, the room went silent.

I looked back to discover that the monsignor of the Catholic Diocese had walked on stage. It made all the little boys quiet down. I laughed and made a note to myself to buy a clerical collar before my next speech.

In the meantime, here's a short excerpt from a telephone interview I most assuredly did not do with Perry.

> ME: Hi, Governor Perry. Thanks for taking my call. How're you doing?
> PERRY:
> ME: I'm sorry, sir, I didn't quite catch —
> PERRY: I — well, no, that wasn't it. I —
> ME: Sir?
> PERRY:
> ME: Maybe I'll call back some other time.
> PERRY: Back?

Lunch with Sacramento city manager John Shirey

I sat down to have lunch with City Manager John Shirey for the second time last Wednesday. The first time was several years ago, when he had just come on board as the executive director of the California Redevelopment Association, and I edited a book for the group.

People who've worked with Shirey, who somewhat resembles an elongated version of New York City Mayor Michael Bloomberg, attest to his intelligence and vision. He can also be pretty funny, especially when speaking off the record.

Shirey wants a new arena built, if adequately financed, but has been surprised by how diminished Kings fans' enthusiasm seems now, compared to when he first came to town. He wants to repair Sacramento's infrastructure above and below (and including) the surface, knows how much it will cost (a couple of billion) but notes that the city is barred from doing a bond issue without voter approval. "Besides, the problem with issuing a bond is that you have to pay it back," he tells me after lunch at the Sterling Hotel's newest eatery, Restaurant Thir13en (this isn't a misprint). "And we don't have the money."

If he had his druthers, he'd prefer to see a privately funded, spectacular new performing arts center built in the city rather than spend government dollars, already committed, to fixing up the Sacramento Community Center Theater. Example of his humor: I ask him where he's going to get the money to do the former and he says, "You're in the arts. You go get it!" I'm on it, John.

He thinks Sacramento's "brand" as a city, destination and business environment is still not well developed, and he'd love to create one that attracts corporate headquarters here. He feels that Mayor Kevin Johnson, "who has a magical presence," could be the lightning rod for this effort. "People like meeting him," he says, despite the fact that Johnson cast the sole "no" vote to hire him late last summer. As my friends back in the Bronx would say, John Shirey has claaaaaass.

Jay Schenirer is way busy

Sacramento City Councilman Jay Schenirer calculates that to win election to his 5th district seat in 2010, "I spent 21 months knocking on 25,000 doors and talking to 8,000 people." I do the math and ask how, if he'd knocked on that many doors, he had spoken with only a third of that number of people. "Seventeen thousand weren't home," he says.

He offers this with a very pleasant smile but he isn't remotely joking. Almost everyone who's worked with Schenirer — an education consultant who spent eight years on the board of trustees of the Sacramento Unified School District (he was president for more than three years) — knows he can be witty, that he likes to laugh but that he's an intensely committed doer. "I've heard that I'm kind of serious and aloof," he says — seriously, but warmly.

To hear him tell it, "No one wanted me to win this seat." Schenirer's principal opponent, Patrick Kennedy, was supported by the teachers' and other unions, and by local business people. Darrell Steinberg, president pro tem of the California Senate and a former Sacramento city councilman, supported Schenirer's bid. But incumbent City Councilman Steve Cohen — perhaps feeling Solomonic — threw his support behind both Schenirer and Kennedy.

Business, as a voting bloc, "now loves me," Schenirer says, which comes off as less of a boast than a simple statement of fact. Schenirer is working these days on an education support program called Way Up Sacramento. It's a five-fold effort that includes tutoring services ("WaySmart"), partnerships with the area's four major healthcare systems

("WayFit"), neighborhood revitalization ("WayHome"), job creation ("WayToWork") and nutrition ("WayFresh").

Hearing about all of this in one sitting — even with WayUp's director, Talia Kaufman, along to clarify things — tends to be, you guessed it, way too much. Which is why, in tomorrow's column/blog (clog), we'll drill down a little. If you were to come back for that, that'd be way cool.

April 5, 2012

Yesterday's clog featured Sacramento District 5 Councilman Jay Schenirer unveiling his WayUp program. While he initially introduced the five-part effort to his constituents, all of its components — tutoring, job creation, nutrition, neighborhood renewal and healthcare — could produce long-term positives for the city.

Education is Schenirer's reason for being (I'd have written that it was his raison d'être, but Thursday is too late in the week to be pretentious). In addition to his City Council work, weighted heavily with youth programs, he's an education consultant whose big-name clients that include the James Irvine Foundation, The California Endowment ("The" must always be capitalized, a former director once told me) and the William and Flora Hewlett Foundation. His partners at Capitol Impact LLC are West Sac Mayor Chris Cabaldon and Rick Miller, who heads up several education policy groups.

Schenirer has been married for 29 years to Bina Lefkovitz, herself a formidable presence in youth development programs for many years. "She volunteers just about full-time with me these days," Schenirer says, grinning. They have two grown sons — David, a sophomore at American University in Washington DC, and Noah, a senior at McClatchy High School — and live in Curtis Park.

"The WayUp program is very scalable," he says. "It can be done anywhere, not just in my district." That's already the case. Schenirer and his aide, Talia Kaufman, who directs the WayUp program, have already hosted the first go-round of Summer At City Hall, which saw 34 students, principally from the Oak Park and Meadowview neighborhoods, doing internships in the city's police department, mayor's office and any other division that volunteered.

Schenirer reels off several of the WayUp Program's success stories and seems particularly proud of a young Latino student, Marlon Lara, whom Kaufman says "is a born grass-roots organizer" from the Woodbine neighborhood. "He's headed to Stanford next year," Schenirer adds.

The WayFit element of the WayUp program teaches kids about jobs in the healthcare industry and aims to provide free health screenings for 1,500 under-served children. The program is a rare partnership among Sutter Health, UC Davis Health System, Kaiser Permanente and Dignity Health (nee Catholic Health Care West, nee Mercy Health Care).

"Aims to provide" are key words in the prior paragraph. In the WayUp brochure, a final column reveals that for all five of its components to work, Schenirer and company need to raise about $265,000. "We're always looking for money," Schenirer says, "from the minute we wake up in the morning."

Ari Fleischer on Obama's chances

A ri Fleischer is on the line from his home office in Westchester County, NY. He says the weather's been "unbelievably beautiful" there this winter. "I think someone's setting us up," he says. It may or may not be a reference to climate change but, delivered in a warm voice (you can actually hear him smiling), it's one of the more offbeat weather predictions I've heard in a long time.

Fleischer, the former White House press secretary and main spokesguy for former President George W. Bush, is coming to town Monday, April 16 under the aegis of "The Cultural Series" launched by Orangevale's Temple Or Rishon. He and Paul Begala, who was a confidant of former President Bill Clinton, will take the stage at 8 p.m. at the Scottish Rite Temple (6151 H St.) to talk politics (what else? You don't go see these guys for cooking demonstrations). Tickets are available at $55 a pop for adults and $25 for students at www.culturalseries.com or by calling (916) 988-4100. There's also a rub-elbows dinner at 6 p.m. for $125 per person.

"I think the timing of the event is great," says Fleischer, who runs a self-named communications firm that advises businesses and professional sports teams. He's also a regular political analyst for CNN, which built a small studio for him in his house. "The Republican nomination (campaign) should be over by that time. President Obama will be attacking Mitt Romney and Romney will be attacking back." Fleischer says he thinks the presidential race is going to be "very tight — like 50/50. The biggest factor will be unemployment, and that's why it's important to keep your eye on the first Friday of each month" (when national

147

unemployment figures are announced). "If unemployment ticks down, it'll put wind in Obama's back. If not, well ... "

Despite his political-star-studded background — he was also the national spokesman and communications director for Elizabeth Dole when she made a short-lived bid for the presidential nomination in 1999 — Fleischer says he's never met the current president. Refreshingly, he doesn't refer to him disrespectfully, even though he points out that he won the presidency "because of the anti-Bush mood in the country in 2008. Obama caught magic in a bottle. But he invented the magic and invented the bottle." It's a practiced bit of phrasemaking but delivered genially.

"I really don't do any active political work these days," says the man who was dubbed "Ari-Bob" during his years with the relentlessly nicknaming Dubya (why, there's one, as well). He says that he enjoys telling people "what it was like to be Jewish in the Bush White House. It was a wonderfully open place. I think that surprises some people."

Asked his age, Fleischer, who's 51, says, "Well, this is how I calculate it. I started working in the White House when I was 40 and I left it three years later. At 65." It's a funny line and catches me off-guard. I think someone was setting me up.

Steve Swatt's new life

" **I** 'll admit I'm old-school," says Steve Swatt, longtime political reporter, analyst and advocate (not all at once) as we sit down at Temple Coffee on S Street. The staff is moving at a glacial pace this particular morning and Swatt finally gives up standing in line as those who precede him discuss their orders ad nauseam with the barista. On some mornings, you could grow, pick and ship the damn beans in the time it takes to order coffee here.

"Channel 3 was very good to me but I could see the industry was changing," Swatt says. "The pie had shrunk in terms of viewers and TV had become a popularity contest. Being the best news station, and the most responsible, suddenly wasn't as important as being number one in the ratings. Crime, sex and celebrity (stories) became all that mattered."

I've known Swatt and his work for years. My late wife, Jane, who worked as a reporter and weekend anchor for Channel 3 from 1978-81, all but idolized him, and I was very OK with that. Swatt was and is a natural teacher (which he proved during a multi-year stint at Sac State). A former staffer for United Press International, the once ubiquitous wire service, as well as the San Francisco Examiner, he covered the trial of Sirhan Sirhan, the busboy who shot to death Robert F. Kennedy in 1968, the night Kennedy won the California primary and was arguably poised to grab, from the late Eugene McCarthy, the Democratic Party's nomination for president. Hubert Horatio Humphrey, Jr., Lyndon B. Johnson's brilliant but hapless veep, then got the nod by default — and came somewhat close to beating Richard M. Nixon for the presidency. But Humphrey, despite being the architect of the fabled war on poverty and a great civil rights advocate in his own right, couldn't overcome his affiliation with Johnson, by then seen as the CEO of the Vietnam War.

Swatt is the last of a breed — a TV journalist who reported on and actually understood policy issues. Now in his 60s — but looking barely different than he looked in his broadcasting heyday (except for the now-absent pitch-black sideburns) — he "put in 23 years" as a reporter before he got "fed up with" television news and went to work for one of the state's premier lobbying firms.

Tomorrow: The "big plans" Swatt swatted away — and his novel approach to semi-retirement.

May 15, 2012 Tuesday

Former Channel 3 reporter, lobbyist and occasional on-air elections analyst Steve Swatt said that United Press International, the late news service for which he reported, had some big plans for him.

Working in Los Angeles in the late 1960s, he handled some of the biggest stories of the day, even covering the trial in Los Angeles of Sirhan Sirhan, Robert F. Kennedy's assassin. But "Whenever a big political story came up, they'd fly in someone from UPI's Sacramento bureau," he tells me over coffee last week. (See yesterday's clog for the first part of this interview.)

"I kept telling (my bosses) I wanted to cover politics, that I understood it, that I'd made some great contacts. So they finally took me aside and said if I just stuck with the job, in about three years I could be a bureau chief — in Albuquerque. I told them, 'I don't want to be a bureau chief and I sure don't want to be one in New Mexico.' So I quit without a job waiting for me."

He ended up connecting with the late Bob Kelly, co-owner with his brother Jon of KCRA-TV Channel 3. Kelly was impressed with Swatt's reporter creds but suggested he go to a smaller TV market, specifically Chico, to learn about the medium. "Bob said, 'Look, you're a news gatherer, not a performer. TV requires you to be both.' I said, 'With all due respect, I'm not going to Chico.' And to my complete surprise, he hired me."

That ability to stand his ground has served Swatt well. He's interviewed governors, presidents and local politicos (he still chats with people on-air for Comcast). No one ever refuses to be interviewed by him because he approaches everyone with respect and a deceptively boyish curiosity. I ask him if, when his and wife Susie's son Jeff was growing up, the boy was impressed with the fact that his father was on TV interviewing major newsmakers. "I think he was impressed when Ronald Reagan signed a picture of them together. I'd taken Jeff to a few of my interviews. But by and large, his attitude was, 'Daddy's job's no big deal.'"

Swatt has been filling his semi-retirement with a number of volunteer projects. But he's also done what nearly every newsperson claims as a dream: he's written a novel, "Fair, Balanced and Dead," about his experiences (available online from amazon.com and bookstore.trafford.com). As I write this, I've read only a third of the book — but because it's largely set in Sacramento, and concerns the adventures of a crusading TV reporter, it's not too challenging to figure out who's who or at least who's a recognizable (and satirical) composite of some familiar local anchors, reporters and politicians. Albuquerque will never know what it missed.

Mediator and storyteller
Joe Genshlea

"I've been a trial lawyer for 45 years," Joe Genshlea says over lunch at Frank Fat's restaurant. "I didn't want to retire. I wanted to keep my skills in play and do something that used all of my experience." And that's why the co-founder of Weintraub Genshlea Chediak Tobin & Tobin is re-branding himself as Joe The Mediator.

That's literally what he calls himself on his new brochure, which ought to give you an idea of his personality. He has a sense of mischief and is confident enough to enjoy poking fun at himself. Example: According to his official bio, he "placed 5,411th in the 83rd running of the Boston AA Marathon."

Genshlea is now "of counsel" to Weintraub — meaning he's still affiliated with the firm and has an office in its 400 Capitol Mall suite, but he's free to pursue his own business interests. "I mediated cases from time to time for other attorneys and really enjoyed it," he says. "Mediation rarely drags on: People generally enter into it because they want to settle a dispute." Since informally announcing his new practice a couple of months ago, Genshlea says he's already mediated six matters.

I ask him if mediation gets the adrenaline pumping as much as going to trial. He smiles and for a brief moment looks wistful. "Now, there's nothing like the feeling you get when you win a jury verdict," he says, recalling his four decades as one of the state's highly respected litigators. "But mediating can be very satisfying. I mean, most cases ought to be settled before they ever get to court, anyway." He says his job "is to listen to both sides, let them know I understand what's at stake, let them know I empathize, then make one or both of them realize that if their case goes forward they're going to lose. Because of my background, I have some credibility if I say to a lawyer, and always with a smile, 'You do realize you're going to get your ass kicked in court, right?'"

Tomorrow: Joe The Mediator is also Joe The Storyteller.

July 12, 2012

As I discussed in yesterday's column, trial attorney Joe Genshlea has become Joe The Mediator. During a four-decade career, Genshlea has represented plaintiffs and defendants in matters ranging from accounting malpractice to toxic mold, trade secrets to personal injury, malicious prosecution to commercial contracts.

People who haven't watched him in court — where he takes an almost avuncular storytelling approach to even the most complicated issues — got a glimpse of his personal style when he presented two popular one-man shows here to raise money for the Sacramento Theatre Company ("A Sense of Place" in 2009) and Sierra Forever Families ("Son of 'A Sense of Place'" in 2011), both of which I helped him put together, the second of which I more-or-less directed (I say "more-or-less" because one simply doesn't tell a 6'2" litigator what to do). While both of the shows were, on the surface, oral memoirs about growing up in Sacramento, they were also wide-ranging, sometimes moving and often hilarious commentaries on politics, culture and, yes, the law.

My favorite story was about a family that goes on vacation and entrusts a neighbor to keep an eye on the house while they're away. The neighbor doesn't notice when a burglar gets into the home. When the family returns, they

153

want to blame the neighbor. The neighbor wants to blame the family for not having locked up the house. Genshlea asked his audience to decide who was ultimately to blame. After a suitable pause he raised his eyebrow and his strong Irish tenor voice with comic indignation. "The burglar!"

Those neighbors should have called Joe The Mediator.

Joe Coomes turns 80

Tomorrow, while cruising the notorious Drake Passage between Antarctica and South America, my friend Joe Coomes will turn 80. He's 18 years my senior and the youngest man I've ever known.

Joe, who's of counsel at Best Best & Krieger and is one of the most respected land-use, redevelopment and public-law attorneys in California, was raised in Yuba City. But that hasn't prevented him from becoming what Claude Rains called Humphrey Bogart's character in "Casablanca" — a citizen of the world. He and his sparkling wife Holly, who passed away almost two years ago, made friends in Boston (where Joe was a visiting professor at MIT), Tibet, England, France, Russia and the most foreign destination imaginable, Texas.

Earlier this year he went on a photo safari in Africa. And two weeks before his trip to Antarctica, he took two of his grandchildren, and their parents, to Washington, DC.

While Joe and I had been friends a long time, it was when my wife Jane lay dying — and a few years later, when Holly, one of Jane's best pals, did the same — that our relationship took on a different, richer, deeper and sadder tone. We were each there for each other during the darkest days of our marriages; as widowers, we share the horrible secret of what it means to watch the love of your life fade away before your eyes.

Joe's made a much better go of widowhood than I have.

Somehow, he's remained upbeat, forward looking and still interested in damn near everything. This is the kind of guy who, as I joked at a memorial service for Holly, writes corrective notes in the margins of physics books. (At least I think I was joking.) We have lunch or dinner once or twice a month and I come away from each meal a little wiser and a little more optimistic about this peculiar negotiation we call life.

I'd be happy to recount all of the milestones and awards in Joe's career but you can find some of those at his law firm's website, others by Googling his name, and most by mentioning him to people in the region-corporate CEOs, mayors, governors, Congresspeople he's advised and the many, many lawyers he mentored along the way.

Joe is known for a mind as fastidious as his desk has never been, his weakness for little cigars and his relentless curiosity. When he sees this, he may just feel compelled to correct it (gently) and send it back to me. And that's just fine. Young guys are always doing that to geezers like me.

Carol Delzer: When the Valentine's Day cards stop

"**P**eople want to tell someone their stories but no one wants to hear them," Carol Delzer says over lunch at Biba Restaurant. "I do. I want to hear everything."

In fact, people tell Delzer things they wouldn't dream of telling someone else. She projects both an aura of warmth and an interest in people that can't be faked, at least not for long. She's an attorney, a certified family-law specialist and a licensed marriage and family therapist. She's also an author and principal of the Family Law Center, whose motto is "Divorce Done Differently." (I can vouch for her truth in advertising, having been a client of hers sometime back.)

About 40 years ago, she was the youngest real estate broker in the region to have her own firm. She listed and sold the largest number of homes here in 1977 and 1978. At one point, in her 20s, Delzer owned 50 houses. She hired her mom, now deceased, to work for her after her dad died.

In short, the vivacious Delzer is a lifelong overachiever. And she feels that her law-and-mediation career brings together all of her skills. "I'm very service oriented," she says. "I don't save many marriages but I do get to ask whose idea it was to get married in the first place, why he or she thought it was a good idea and whose idea it was to get a divorce."

Delzer says that most people view the so-called permanent commitment of marriage as "an enhancer of their relationship. But marriage draws out everything we have and are. It's not always the right answer for everyone."

While Delzer has associate attorneys at her firm, "If people call and want to see me, that's who they'll see. I'm very hands-on and (I recognize that) just showing up at a meeting to plan your divorce is stressful. You think the lawyer is judging you. But that's not my role. It's to help ease people through one of the most difficult transitions in their lives."

Tomorrow, we'll look at some of Delzer's books. Spoiler alert: She's been divorced, too.

Feb. 15, 2013

As we learned yesterday, the motto of attorney-mediator Carol Delzer's law office is "Divorce Done Differently." So it should come as no surprise that she'll have a book out this spring called "Divorce Made Easier." Or that she, herself, has been divorced — twice, in fact.

"My first marriage ended in 1989, the year I finished law school and passed the bar — so some good came out of it," she says with a wide smile over lunch at Biba Restaurant. A dedicated golfer, she uses a links term to describe a second, relatively brief marriage, which also ended in divorce. "I think of that as a Mulligan," she says. (For non-golfers — and that would include me — a Mulligan is a do-over shot.) "He was a Methodist minister, a really good guy. It just didn't work out."

Delzer says she first became interested in mediating divorces, instead of working exclusively as a divorce lawyer, in law school. "We were being trained to be position-oriented," she says. "You had to take your client's side, see things from the client's point of view. I thought that was fine, but it wasn't me, or at least not all of me. I wanted to help people — and their children."

In fact, Delzer's other two books to date are "8 Weeks to Collaborative Co-Parenting for Divorcing Parents," of which she's the sole author, and "Positive Discipline for Single Parents," of which she's a co-author. You can buy them online at her website or pick up a free copy by dropping into her offices at 1722 Professional Drive in Sacramento.

A slim, stylish woman with dark hair, Delzer dresses like someone who isn't, as the fashionistas say, afraid of color. When she's not mediating, writing or golfing, she's an enthusiastic consumer of the arts — and, better yet, a financial supporter and volunteer, proving that while she may specialize in divorce, she's far from afraid of commitment.

March 21, 2013

Meet new Roseville mayor Susan Rohan

"The next time I enter a contest, I'm going to make sure I know what the prize is," Susan Rohan says, her tongue steadfastly lodged in her cheek.

Over coffee at Sammy's Rockin' Island Bar & Grill, she's just run through a laundry list of her duties as the city of Roseville's mayor. That's the "contest" she won when she was the top vote getter in the 2010 city council election. According to Roseville rules, that person goes into office as vice-mayor for the first two years, then ascends to the top job in the final years of the four-year term.

"People expect their mayor to be responsive to requests as varied as supporting a resolution on behalf of Eagle Scouts to (attending) the dedication of the restoration of a 110-year-old church," she says. Rohan estimates she spends a bit more than 30 hours a week in her allegedly part-time job.

She appears to love it.

Roseville lost a good deal of momentum during the recession, in terms of commercial development, residential real estate, retail and services. The resurrection of its downtown, as personified by Vernon Street — a charming stretch of small-town America with modest metropolitan aspirations — started to seem doubtful.

Yet this afternoon, after the lunch crowd has thinned, the street is still quietly, steadily bustling. There are shops and restaurants, the historic Tower Theatre and the thriving Blue Line Arts — the once-traditional art gallery that's been reinventing itself as an all-arts nonprofit organization. It recently managed to kidnap the Sacramento region's

160

prestigious Crocker-Kingsley Show, a national, juried art exhibit. In fact, Rohan has just joined its volunteer board of directors. (In candor, I'm on it, too.)

"I love what's happening here on Vernon Street," Her Honor says, "but people who know me get that I'm not interested in doing things just for cosmetic value. I want economic results." She looks around Sammy's, a popular new restaurant-bar-club, figure-headed by singer Sammy Hagar but developed by local entrepreneurs (whom I'll be writing about in the next few weeks). "I do have a soft spot for nostalgia, though," she says. She reminds me that Sammy's used to be a JCPenney store. "And now," she says, "it's a gathering place for businesspeople, officials and tourists."

Tomorrow, the mayor opens up about her background and the Sacramento Kings. "I understand it's a basketball team," she says, tongue returned in cheek.

March 22, 2013

"If you live in Placer County, not just look at it on a map, you kind of erase the boundary lines separating Roseville, Rocklin, Loomis and Lincoln," says Roseville Mayor Susan Rohan in a mid-afternoon interview at Sammy's Rockin' Island Bar & Grill. We're just down the block from Roseville's impressive civic center complex, which was built a little more than a decade ago, on the town's steadily reviving Vernon Street.

Rohan is a big believer in regional cooperation and speaks highly of the work being done under the Next Economy rubric to unite the Sacramento area's counties and, more important, its communities. I ask her if she has a position on the value of keeping the Sacramento Kings here. She gets an elfin look on her face and says, all innocence, "The Kings? I understand it's a basketball team."

After we both laugh, she says, "I'm not at all into sports but it's very important for us to hang onto the Kings. The team brings value to the entire region."

"In some ways," Rohan says, "Roseville and the other towns around us remind me of the little Nebraska town I grew up in, Hartington, except that only had a population of 1,100. As you can imagine, it was closely knit. My mom's 83 and has lived there since 1959. She's considered one of 'the new ones.'

"But youth programs, sports, the churches and the schools in the area unite everyone," she continues. "Again, there are no boundary lines."

Rohan thinks the city council has done "a very good job of listening to what the community wants," as it moves ahead to redevelop its downtown and, a few blocks away, its historic district. "Take this block, for instance. When we approved this place, Sammy's, we had to ask ourselves if we were planning to create a gaslight district, with clubs and restaurants open late. But the community owns the vision. It's our job as council members to just make it happen. And we knew — and people told us — that a gaslight district wouldn't fit the community. We wanted to create an area with complementary experiences." Sammy's stops rockin' at midnight.

The mayor's background qualifies her more than most local officials to make land use decisions. When she's not spending 30-plus hours on city business, Rohan is a public affairs consultant. She was vice president of governmental and environmental affairs for Del Webb, posted at the retirement community giant's Lincoln offices. She said her "job of a lifetime" was when she worked for Tenneco Realty in Bakersfield (which was purchased by Castle & Cooke in the late 1980s). There, she was director of residential development.

"I have a degree in English and history, so naturally I ended up in property acquisition and building," she says, grinning at her the seeming non sequitur of her training and career. In fact, her first job out of college had her working the lumber business, which is where her organizational skills caught the eye of the Tenneco people.

Rohan is married to Einar Maisch, director of strategic affairs for the Placer County Water Agency. They live on the east side of Roseville and have, she says, "a beautifully blended family" of grown children, grandchildren at least one step-grandchild. She says that they all spend holidays together, spouses and ex-spouses, "and it's wonderful."

Proving this public servant knows how to erase all kinds of boundaries.

HUMAN FRAILTIES

Doctors see right through me

These days, my back goes out more often than I do. According to research, both scientific and anecdotal, I'm not alone in this. You probably have back trouble, too, at least sometimes. You probably do or have done physical therapy. You've maybe dieted and tried acupuncture, chiropractic or meditation in the hope that one of them would provide the panacea. Perhaps you've met with your religious leader — or even tried to make deals with your religious leader's Ultimate Boss: "I promise to worship regularly if you'll just let me pull on my socks in under an hour."

My back trouble isn't predictable. I'm sometimes amazed at how many boxes I can schlep from my garage to my basement without once experiencing pain (or, for that matter, a sense of why I'm schlepping these boxes in the first place). At other times, I'll simply walk into my kitchen and suddenly feel an invisible knife slicing its way up and down my left side. (Amateur psychologists need not apply: Entering my kitchen isn't causing the pain. I love to cook. Doing the dishes, on the other hand....)

I was thinking about all of this last week when my sciatica started acting up and I went to get my back X-rayed at one of the 7,000 clinics run by Radiological Associates of Sacramento within a 12-block radius. It's possible I'm inflating those numbers; but in the past decade, as a caregiver and then as a patient, I've been inside more RAS clinics than, perhaps, some of the radiologists. I've watched or experienced scans done using magnetic resonance imaging, positron emission tomography and computerized axial tomography and — respectively, MRIs, PETs and CTs, which are also called CATs in the misguided hope they'll sound cute.

I've held my hands above my head as I was x-rayed, and tightly at my side when I was scanned. Last week I was asked to cross my hands over my chest for a shot or two but I told the lab tech this felt a bit funereal, even though I was standing up. She rolled her eyes and I realized she held all the cards: I wasn't about to lam out of the building in an open-backed hospital gown. So if you happened to be in the vicinity of 28th and L Streets at the time, she's the one you need to thank. And maybe that Ultimate Boss.

April 12, 2012

We need a new word — "manxiety"?

I'd like to add a word to the ongoing unification of language as it pertains to the sexes: Manxiety. I realize the root word "anxiety" contains nothing gender-specific, at least not as far as I can tell (but then, I'm a guy and we apparently tend to skip the nuances and head straight to the sports bar). So why am I suggesting the creation of a gender-specific term?

Because I have never met a man who admitted to having an anxiety attack. I've never met one who, in a clutch moment, said, "I feel somewhat anxious." In fact, I know very few men who even say "somewhat."

We men go ballistic, postal and bananas but we don't suffer from "angst" (a word that comes from the Danish "dread" — two words that suggest an even stranger condition, fear of pastry).

We men get impatient but we don't get hyper. We're enthusiastic but never eager. We do edgy but not irritable. We think things are cool, but hardly ever lovely.

We get annoyed but we don't get antsy. And even though we've been wearing pants longer than women have, we never get ants in them.

So in a world that seems increasingly willing to embrace the terms "manopause" and "pre-manstral" syndrome, each respectively denoting a change of life and a swing of mood, why can't we come right out and admit that most men get afraid, nervous and silly sometimes, i.e., anxious?

About a year ago I went through a spell (OK, a period, if you'd like) during which my nerves were shot from quitting cold-turkey some prescription drugs I'd begun to love a little too much during two years of surgeries. As my body reacclimated itself, I'd occasionally freak out (OK, panic like a little girl) if I had to make a long drive somewhere. I found my eyes welling up while watching certain movies or even TV commercials.

Let's face it: I was manxious. I had manxiety. I suffered from mangst. But I'm better now. So pass me that pastry.

May 4, 2012

Early risers they aren't

If you have children or grandchildren in their teens or 20s, or just deal with people of that age, perhaps you'll understand my dubbing them Generation Zzzz. This is, by far, the best-rested group of people in our country's history.

There may be some jealousy at play here. For a variety of reasons, even if I don't climb into bed until 3 a.m., I seem constitutionally incapable of sleeping past 6:30 or 7 a.m., at least as a general rule. I like to flatter myself into thinking it's because my mind is just aflame with creativity and won't permit me to fritter away the morning abed. (Note: "abed" is not the past tense of "Abe." Rather, it's one of those great New York Times crossword puzzle words that are never used in actual conversation.)

But it's not really that. I just get tired of being tired — and suspect that if I don't jump out of the sack while it's still relatively early in the day, I'm going to miss something. (At my age, I'm not really sure what that might be. For years, it was probably Diane Sawyer.)

I can't tell you how many young people I know or are related to — one even calls me Dad — who, given the opportunity, can sleep until noon, or even later. Granted, these young people aren't eating senior-citizen dinners at 4:30 p.m. and heading off to bed by 9; in fact, most of the ones I know go out to dinner or start their TV viewing at 11 p.m. or later, so it makes sense that their body clocks, after working the graveyard shift, would unwind while the rest of us are just settling in with NPR's "All Things Considered" (which gets started around 3:30 p.m. in Sacramento — and, unfortunately, has yet to consider this vitally important topic).

To be fair, many of the young people I'm referring to, particularly the one who insists on calling me Dad, are forced or choose to burn their candles at both ends. My daughter Jessica and her husband Joshua, for example, are theater people but work during the day. This schedule doesn't allow them to sleep in all that often-but when there's a break in the action (e.g., most playhouses are closed on Mondays) they're capable of making up for lost time.

Maybe I should dub them the Lost Time Generation.

May 22, 2012

Agitated? Who's agitated?

When I was about 9 years old, my Uncle Moishe took me to breakfast one day and insisted I order a cup of hot chocolate. "Eddie," he told me as I began to sip, "they say that if you drink cocoa for 99 years, you'll live long." I didn't realize for a few days what a funny remark that was. But I certainly thought about it when the findings came out last week indicating that drinking coffee may help you live longer.

According to a researcher at the National Cancer Institute, it doesn't matter if your preference is full-throttle (regular) or neutered (decaf). Either one may offer "a modest benefit." For those of us who consume several cups of the hard stuff every day — even after 3 p.m., or whenever that moment occurs that makes insomnia inevitable — the news was difficult to process. Perhaps it's because many of us read the article in the afternoon and were so jittery we couldn't focus.

My own tendency, when overly caffeinated, is to unintentionally skip several words in an article I'm reading. Example: "Coffee contains a thousand things that can affect health" (a direct quote from the Associated Press story) becomes, in my agitated mind, "Coffee contains health." I'm also aware that drinking coffee before I get a medical exam is a bad idea since it can raise blood pressure and one's LDL (bad cholesterol). By the way, there's also a new finding that the so-called "good" cholesterol isn't all that great, either, when it starts to escalate.

I feel like the guy in the old joke who says he's been reading so much about the bad effects of smoking that he's decided to give up reading.

So: How much coffee do you drink? Please pop me an email (use the link above). And don't worry about what time you send it. I'm sure I'll be up.

Another alarming study

Y ou may need to sit down to hear this. Or maybe you shouldn't. A startling new study, if you happen to startle easily, reveals that sitting may be bad for you. Not just sitting in front of the television, especially if it's on, but also sitting at your desk, at live performances, and, while the study didn't mention it, I'm going to add in front of firing squads and oncoming trains.

The study's stunning outcome suggests that if we exercise more and sit less we might live longer (or it might just seem longer). And here are a few activities the study finds acceptable as part of an overall exercise program: placing your trash can "on the other side of the office" — presumably so you have to arc your free-throw a little more when you're tossing away hard copies of studies — as well as "standing during coffee breaks and telephone calls...."

The study was conducted at the University of Queensland and reviewed by, I'm fairly certain, a standing committee. So what does this tell us — other than that Australian colleges, just like their counterparts here in the U.S., know how to secure grants to conduct knuckleheaded studies?

My favorite findings from the study involve what I call oxymoronic statistics. In 2008, Australian adults "viewed a collective 9.8 billion hours of television," according to the New York Times account of the study. OK. Now combine that with this factoid, also part of the study: "Every single hour of television watched after the age of 25 reduces the viewer's life expectancy by 21.8 minutes." Am I missing a narrative thread?

I always urge my marketing clients to avoid using oxymoronic statistics like the above when promoting their companies. For example, you should never put in a brochure or on your website that your firm "has a combined 386 years of business law experience." To be sure, that could be an interesting number — if you had a three-person firm. But if you have 128 in-house attorneys, this might not be as impressive. It means each of your lawyers has been practicing, on average, for a little more than three years.

Also, what difference does your firm's "combined" experience make? Is every attorney in the firm going to be working on every single case?

I think I'll pause here, flip on the news and shorten my life. G'day!

Mom and Pop, stop!

I f you're still paying your kid's college costs and you're not happy about it, cheer up. A new national study reveals that the more generous you are, the lower Junior's grades are going to be. When I was a mere lad living in the candor capital of the world, New York City, we had an expression for this: "You're off the hook!"

To recap: If you want your child's GPA to improve, just cut him or her off.

I find it interesting that a sociology professor from nearby UC Merced is the author of the study. I'd expect that a professor in a state better known for harshness than we are (like New York, Texas or Alaska) would have conducted and published this research. After all, in the land of stereotypes, we're supposed to be the "nanny state," a population of insatiable coddlers and cuddle-bunnies who'd do anything for our kids — except provide them with gritty values to prepare them for the fabled real world.

According to the New York Times, the professor, Laura Hamilton, "suggested that students who get a blank parental check may not take their education as seriously as others."

Is this manna from the heavens of academia, or what? And can you imagine how happy Dr. Hamilton's colleagues, dean and chancellor must be with her for inspiring a deluge of student aid requests?

What the study doesn't include is helpful data for parents who find themselves paying their kids' college costs even though the kids graduated some years back. This probably feels somewhat akin to making monthly alimony payments even though you've remarried but your ex-spouse has wisely opted not to follow suit.

Less harshly — after all, I do live in a nanny state — it must seem like making payments on a big-screen television whose technology was completely out of date before you paid it off. Or on a car that spends more time in the shop than the mechanic does. Either way, let's call it delayed grad-ification.

AUTHORS, ARTISTS AND ENTERTAINERS

Dec. 20, 2011

Valerie Weinberg's inspiring life story

My friend Valerie Weinberg is a wonderfully expressive jazz vocalist, a well-connected concert promoter, a tireless booking agent and, to any woman who's ever been discouraged from pursuing her dream, downright inspirational.

Weinberg sings as Valerie V (an adaptation of her family name, Levy, pronounced levee). She'll perform on the main concourse of Terminal B from 6-8 p.m. on Thursday, at the place I call Sacramento Unintentional Airport (motto: "Just try to park within an hour! Mmwahaha!").

On New Year's Eve, she'll sing at Thunder Valley Casino's High Steaks restaurant (the Beach Boys will be performing in the same building). She's already lined up a number of 2012 gigs for her and the musicians she represents.

Thunder Valley is in Lincoln. It isn't a far drive from Granite Bay, where Val and her husband, Jerrold, raised their three children: twin sons Corey and David, 23, and daughter Lauren, 19. Corey's currently interning at Assemblyman Chris Norby's office, David on the Miami Dolphins' press staff. Lauren's working on a degree in broadcast journalism at the University of Arizona. In summary, achievement seems to be a family tradition.

But Granite Bay was a lifetime away. She wanted to become a professional singer but instead was the kind of wife and mom who always surprises everyone at community talent shows, holiday gatherings and local fundraisers by having a voice and stage presence well beyond amateur status.

"I loved raising my children," she says, "but I felt as though I was drowning. I knew if I didn't make a change I'd regret it for the rest of my life." She moved to a place a few blocks from the family's home. Today, she's single, busy and remains close to her kids.

On-stage, Valerie V comes across as a lanky, stylish interpreter of the great American jazz and pop songbook. She's currently working with her accompanist, Chet Chwalik, to prepare a Barbra Streisand tribute set, which she hopes to take on tour. Don't doubt it will happen. In her late 50s, this is a person at the cusp of her career-a woman who escaped her own silent environment to become herself.

Tim Comstock has murder on his mind

I'm sharing a hot dog, literally, with a hardboiled crime novelist who's wearing a Hawaiian shirt and calling our selection "a diet dog. Relish counts as a vegetable, right?" While Tim Comstock is mild-mannered, his first work of fiction, "Reunion in Carmel," is anything but. It's a gripping, violent-but-sensitive noir whose style, for me, is a combination of Elmore Leonard (Pulp Fiction) and John D. MacDonald (the Travis McGee series).

When Comstock and I meet for lunch at The Wienery at 56th and H Streets, I tell him how impressed I was with his book (which he'd given me a copy of the previous time I ran into him at The Wienery). He's been told how good a writer he is but the news still seems to surprise and delight him. "Listen, I had to take dumbbell English" when he was a history student at UC Berkeley. "To this day, I couldn't diagram a sentence if my life depended on it." I tell him a lot of us who write for a living would be dead under those conditions, which seems to cheer him immensely.

"Reunion in Carmel" is about a serial killer who, through circumstances that would require me to issue several spoiler alerts, shows up in lovely Carmel-By-The-Sea on a mission of revenge. In the book's marvelously deceptive introduction, Comstock writes that the events depicted in the book "occurred nearly 15 years ago," which becomes part of the book's charm for me. The events never occurred anywhere but in Comstock's imagination. It's similar to the conceit of the low-budget/high-octane film "The Blair Witch Project," which purports to be a semi-documentary.

Ed Goldman: But I Digress ...

Comstock, who's a very lively 65, was the dean of
students at California State University Sacramento for 19
years, which is where he met Don Yelverton, the late chief
of police of the campus, who became the model for Phil
Curry, one of the book's more memorable characters. Since
Comstock and his family spend a good deal of time in Carmel
— his family has owned a small home there since the 1920s,
which Tim and his late brother Bill remodeled in the 1990s
— I ask if the crime rampage he recounts in the book has any
basis in fact. "It's not based on anything," he says, smiling
widely. "You should read the Carmel police reports. The
biggest thing that happens there is when someone's cat gets
caught in a tree."

He sips his soda. "That's why I set the book there," he
says. "I wanted to see what would happen if I put the worst
stuff possible in a setting so beautiful and peaceful."

Tomorrow: In Tim Comstock's world, death takes no
holidays.

April 25, 2012

In slightly saltier language, Tim Comstock says his wife
of 42 years, Nancy, told him, "Don't you let anything
happen to those kids! You hear me?" She wasn't referring
to the couple's grown sons: Tim, 38, a Realtor, or Will, 33,
a bar manager at the Courtyard by Marriott in downtown
Sacramento. Instead, she was looking out for two of the
young characters in her husband's debut novel, "Reunion in
Carmel."

The book, as I rhapsodized about it yesterday, is a
gripping, violent crime story. Its setting, in one of the
state's more scenic and placid villages, serves as an effective
counterpoint to what is, in essence, a dark tale of revenge.

Sacramento-based artist Miles Hermann created the evocative cover.

Over lunch at The Wienery, Comstock admits that he's never seen, at least in person, any of the lurid crime scenes he so skillfully depicts in Reunion. "I'm just a guy who grew up in the suburbs," he says. "I never saw the awful stuff I wrote about." On the other hand, he grew up seeing all of the beautiful stuff he writes about when he describes his beloved Carmel — the rapturous but unforgiving ocean, the dense and damp foliage, the inky night sky.

"The flash of lightning was razor-true," the book begins, "sending the top quarter of the huge cypress crashing to the beach below. A cannonade of sparks was quickly extinguished by the driving rain. Seventy feet of the tree remained standing, its humbled form a sad monument to this savage spring storm." This is not the work of an amateur.

"The first thing I wrote and sold," Comstock recalls, "was (a memoir) about caddying for Max Baer," the late fighter, Sacramentan and father of the actor-producer best known for playing Jethro on "The Beverly Hillbillies." Comstock sent the piece to a writer he knew at Sports Illustrated. To his utter shock, he received a check for $1,000 in the self-addressed, stamped envelope freelancers always used to include when they mailed manuscripts they'd written on spec. The article was published in 1984.

"I stared at the check, then at the story when it came out, and thought, 'OK! I'm a writer now! This is what I do! I'm gonna be rich and famous!" That didn't happen — or at least, it hasn't happened yet. Comstock says he has two more books he wants to write. One would be a sequel of sorts to "Reunion in Carmel," the other a devilishly clever thriller involving a presidential advisor who goes on a crime spree. "I picture James Carville," he says, "only a much better looking version of him."

That sounds like a daunting task. But anyone who can make tranquil Carmel-By-The-Sea seem dangerous and foreboding may just be up to it.

April 27, 2012

David Ligon can
make a movie for $100

Fade in: When he started his filmmaking career about six years ago, David Ligon says, "I knew very few actors here. Now I've worked with more than 100 of them. There are some tremendously talented people in Sacramento." Several of them may be seen tonight at 9 when Ligon's 24-minute movie, "Bitter/Sweet," is screened at the Artisan Theater at 1901 Del Paso Blvd. as part of the continuing Sacramento International Film Festival. It's a lovely, lively slice-of-strife comedy-drama that focuses on a coterie of middle-aged empty-nester women whose regular afternoon teas are interrupted by a young woman whose idealism reminds them — bitterly and sweetly, one might say — of their own vanished dreams.

That's pretty heady stuff for a guy who says he just likes to make comedies. "I've always felt that I have a unique style of writing humor," he says earlier this week over a coffee-ish drink that takes longer to order than to drink. We're at the Peet's Coffee and Tea that someone plunked down in a Safeway parking lot in midtown. "My favorite stories don't move along in a linear fashion. I think it makes the films more memorable. Two recent films I loved are 'Scott Pilgrim v. The World' and 'Kickass.' Neither was especially linear."

Ligon grew up in Brentwood — the farming community in Contra Costa County, not the show-biz enclave in Southern California. He holds a bachelor's degree in speech communications from Fresno State and an M.A. in political communications from Sacramento State. "I've never studied filmmaking or taken a writing course in my life," he says.

187

"I think the main reason I love to write dialogue is because I want to see what my characters have to say." He smirks, looks down and mumbles, "And they always make me laugh."

If you follow show business, you already know that two indispensable components in making movies are raising money and spending money. But for independent filmmakers like Ligon — who brings his own high-definition camera, lights, editing software and computer to the enterprise, and engages actors "who do this for no money up-front because they like the scripts and they like having the opportunity to act" — a professional film can sometimes be made "for under $100." He says he'd like to make a full-length feature film but that "I'd need to hire a full crew for that. I just can't get that kind of quality all by myself."

Ligon lives and works in a one-bedroom apartment in midtown. Through his company Ligon Media, he creates advertising and public relations campaigns, and produces industrial and public services videos. I should mention that a 30-second spot he directed for the Sacramento Hospice Consortium is one of the most heart-churning pieces of what we marketing types call "messaging" that I've seen.

In addition to completing a new film, "Ménage á Ted," Ligon says he's been working on a standup comedy act that "I hope to attempt performing in the next year." OK, people, that's a wrap.

Meet double Grammy winner Mary Youngblood

I f you're wondering how to impress a two-time Grammy winner over lunch, do not, repeat, do not, do as I do: In one clumsy move I knock over three full water glasses, drenching musician Mary Youngblood and forcing us to move to another table.

But Youngblood, who's experienced far tougher knocks in her 53 years, takes it in stride. "I'm sure you didn't mean it," she says in the mellow, reassuring voice that may be familiar to you from her CDs, live performances and lectures (and ought to be a staple of talk radio).

While she's also a classically trained pianist and warm-voiced singer, Youngblood may be best known for playing the Native American flute. She has 250 of them in her collection "but only 20 are in pitch," she says. "It's that sensitive an instrument." Her compositions have been highlighted in movies, including 2007's "The Spirit of Sacajawea," and she's performed all over the world. (You can order her albums from amazon.com or keep up with her comings and goings at maryyoungblood.com.)

What you might not know is that she has four children, two grandchildren and lives in Fair Oaks. "It took me a while to feel that Sacramento could be my home," she says. "But about 10 or 15 years ago, something just clicked here for me. I realized I'd grown my family here and that along the way this had become my community."

Her adoptive parents, educators Leah and Robert Edwards, live a mile from her. I ask if they encouraged her to become a musician. "Well, here's what happened," she says. "One evening we were at their friends' home. They had a piano. I was 4 years old and I walked over to it and picked out Petula Clark's song 'Downtown' one note at a time. The friends said, 'Good God! She has talent! Get her lessons.' And that's what happened."

None of Youngblood's children, she says, "has a propensity for music. But that's OK."

I ask Youngblood what it was like to win the Grammy — twice, in different years, even though her category, "Best Native American Music Album" (which no longer exists) was featured in the pre-show ceremony. "It was surreal when they called my name," she says. "I was sitting up close. The Blind Men From Alabama had just won for Best Folk Album. I think it was pretty much as I'd always imagined it would be."

Not long ago, the Grammy board of directors decided to combine 34 kinds of ethnic music into one all-purpose category: "Roots Music." "I understand the thinking but it's just awful," Youngblood says. "I mean, Native Americans make up only one percent of the U.S. population. They obviously figured we just didn't have that demographic draw."

On Monday, as our chat continues, Mary Youngblood talks about finding her birth mother — and our waitress comes up with the best description of the superstar I inadvertently soaked. Please stop by.

May 21, 2012

Years ago, Mary Youngblood — the two-time Grammy winner on which I accidentally knocked the contents of three filled water glasses at lunch last week — was a welfare mom who pretty much created her own career. Her first husband had died of acute alcoholism in his 40s. "It's been a problem for my people," she says; as you may guess, she doesn't drink.

Her birth mother did, however. Youngblood managed to track her down in 1986. "We developed a relationship of sorts," she says, her eyes getting a faraway look for the first and only time during our interview.

With a number of CDs to her credit — and one, "Nuchek Island," on the way next year, she promises (you can keep tabs on her at maryyoungblood.com) — Youngblood is thinking about the next phase of her career. Her haunting music, which features her on the Native American flute (she's also a singer and classically trained pianist), has been used in films and she'd like to do more of that, as well as studio work. "The great part about being a studio musician," she says, "is that while you work with other professionals — and I mean the engineers, not just the musicians — you get to watch your baby being born."

I ask if she's ever considered composing crossover music, to expand beyond the well regarded but smallish niche of Native American music. "I like to think I've always been a cross-over artist," she says. "I'm pretty eclectic. I write and play actual melodies on my (Native American) flute, and I was the first musician I know of to do that." Executives at Silver Wave Records, her onetime label, wanted her albums to emerge from a single theme, she says. "I told them I couldn't do that. Music's just too interesting and important to me to limit it."

These days, Youngblood is planning to write a book about her life, combining it with the poetry she's been writing for most of it. "The lyrics I write for my songs are really just adaptations of my poems," she says.

When our lunch is over, our waitress, who profusely apologized for spilling all that water on Youngblood, even though I'm the only one who did, walks to our table. She's all grins. "I've been listening to your enthusiasm," she tells Youngblood, "and I can see why we had to pour water on you. You're on fire, lady!"

I thank her — not for taking the rap about the spill but for nicely summarizing Mary Youngblood's next chapter.

Claire Mix:
Not your ordinary filmmaker

"**A**s my body grows weaker, my spirit grows stronger," midtown resident Claire Mix tells me. That spirit, accompanied by her formidable skills as a filmmaker and composer, has galvanized her to make one of the most moving and thought-provoking documentaries I've ever seen. Apparently, I'm not the only one who feels this way. The film, "Gila River and Mama: The Ruth Mix Story," is a finalist in the Northern California Emmy Awards, which will be presented Saturday night in San Francisco.

But Mix, who's the director, producer, writer and composer of the film, won't be in the audience. She has Parkinson's disease, first diagnosed 10 years ago. Still in her early 50s, she retired from teaching a few weeks ago. Her mobility is not only limited but also, she says, "pretty unpredictable," which is why I'm interviewing her by phone even though she lives only 13 blocks from me.

"Most of the time I was directing the film, I sat in a wheelchair and had the actors come to me after each 'take,'" she says. Yet watching Mix on-screen (she's one of the testifiers), you wouldn't suspect she's anything but a striking, robust woman. Her eyes are alive with passion for her subject: her late mother, Ruth, who at the age of 15 worked as a nurse's aide at the Gila River internment camp for Japanese Americans during World War II. Ruth's memories of her own mother, Frida, who worked at the horribly dilapidated Arizona facility as a schoolteacher, form the framework of the film. Ruth Mix died, at the age of 78, just a few months after the movie was completed.

I mention to Claire Mix how healthy she looks in her own segments and she reveals some off-camera magic along with charming self-deprecating humor. "What you don't see is that I'm in a wheelchair," she says, "clutching the arms desperately so I won't shake. I sat so rigidly that the crew kidded me and said they could edit my testimony with really bad jump-cuts and my head was so still, you'd never even notice."

The film features interviews with survivors of the facility, which was probably the most photographed internment camp of the war. "My mother and grandmother helped smuggle in rolls of film," Mix says in a playful tone (the movie depicts this). While these testimonials are often heartbreaking, with Mix's elegiac music complementing the soft-spoken sincerity of the interviewees, I found the reenactment scenes, shot in black-and-white and featuring some wonderful young local actors, nearly overwhelming.

You might, too. You can order the film online at gilariverandmama.com. Tomorrow, we'll chat a little more about this extraordinary movie — and its equally extraordinary auteur. Intermission.

June 6, 2012

Ever since I watched the film "Gila River and Mama: The Ruth Mix Story," which has been nominated for a Northern California Emmy Award, and interviewed Claire Mix — its writer, producer, director and composer — I've been trying to figure out why both of the experiences got to me so much. Maybe it's because the film and the filmmaker are equally inspiring.

The film is a nonfiction memory play in which Claire's mother, Ruth Mix, talks about her experiences volunteering as a nurse's aide 70 years ago at Butte Camp Hospital, the under-equipped medical facility at the disgraceful Gila River Japanese internment camp in Arizona. She was there because her late mother, Frida, worked at the camp as a schoolteacher.

Ruth Mix died a few months after shooting her scenes, at 79. Her testimony in the film — as well as interviews with several survivors of the camp and the filmmaker herself — is illuminating, clear-eyed, emotional — and frequently angering.

How could the United States ignore its own Constitution and treat its own citizens so indifferently?

"These were citizens of the United States that were being ignored to death," Ruth says at one point in the film. In another segment, she describes the government's public relations efforts to make it seem as though the prisoners, for that's what they were, were being treated respectfully. "While they were putting a nice face on it, reality was going along, too," Mix says.

As the film and her daughter make clear, Ruth Mix was the only Caucasian nurse's aide at the hospital; the rest of the staff were Japanese-American internees.

"The sadness," says Marielle Tsukomoto, an interviewee, "was overwhelming."

That's true of the film, too. But there is also an undercurrent here of the indomitable spirit of the internees who clung fast to a single concept: perseverance. As I mentioned in yesterday's column, that word also applies to the filmmaker, Claire Mix. She's struggled with Parkinson's disease since first being diagnosed in 2002. When the television academy hands out its Northern California Emmy Awards this Saturday night, I hope it realizes that "Gila River and Mama: The Ruth Mix Story" saw courage happening on both sides of the camera.

How Jeff Knorr became a poet

If your notion of a poet laureate is a white-haired 80-year-old who shows up at presidential inaugurations, royal weddings and state funerals, you haven't met Jeff Knorr, who's just begun a two-year term as Sacramento's poet laureate.

An energetic, down-to-earth college professor and fly-fisherman, Knorr was selected last month by a panel of the Sacramento Metropolitan Arts Commission to be the city and county's official versifier. Over coffee, I ask him to reveal his superhero back story — i.e., how he came to be a poet.

"I'm not really sure," he says. "My mom was a teacher and my dad was an engineer with Southern Pacific Railroad." He clarifies the last part of that sentence: "A civil engineer. He didn't drive the train."

Knorr, who's 46, says he was majoring in biology at Chico State in the hope of someday becoming a forest ranger in Yosemite. "But a professor took me aside and said, 'Listen, you're struggling miserably as a biology major. You're frustrated and frankly, I'm frustrated with you.'" The professor suggested that Knorr spend a semester or two pursuing other interests. "And that was all I needed to see that biology and I weren't meant for each other. I took (courses in) Renaissance history, philosophy, jazz and modern drama."

In an English class, he discovered the experimental poetry of the late James Arlington Wright, whose breakthrough collection, "The Green Wall" won a major prize from Yale University. But Knorr says it was Wright's seminal work, "The Branch Will Not Break," that resonated more. "My now ex-wife gave a copy of it to me as I left for

196

Barcelona," he recalls. "Wright wrote about Spain and was influenced by its culture. It made my trip there more meaningful."

It was in Barcelona that Knorr, who's been teaching English for 20 years, first presided over a classroom. "It was a group of sixth-graders," he says. "I taught homeroom, English, math and history."

Knorr served as chair of the English department at Sacramento City College for nearly three years, where he's taught since 2001. His books of poetry include "The Third Body," "Keeper" and "Standing Up to the Day." He also co-wrote (with Tim Schell) two non-fiction books on writing.

Tomorrow, he tells us what businesspeople can learn from poets — and vice, uh, verse-a.

Sept. 11, 2012

"There's a definite business side to being an artist" says Sacramento's poet laureate, Jeff Knorr. "I tell my creative-writing students that declaring yourself an artist doesn't mean you can miss deadlines. People won't wait for you. They'll go with the next guy, the guy who showed up on time. If you want to be successful as an artist, you'd better learn what it takes to sit at the adults' table."

Knorr says that, similarly, CEOs and CFOs need to appreciate that there's a world outside of business. "It's easy for poets and business people to live in little bubbles," he says. "Poets and business people alike experience rejection along the way and they both succeed by focusing on the task at hand but having a wider vision.

"It's also important for all of us to acknowledge the people who helped us along the way," he continues. "I still get some rejection slips for my poems but it doesn't bother

197

me as it used to. Instead, I think about how lucky I am — and I think about all of the people who encouraged me. That's why I tell my students, as I was told when I was in college, to submit their work to writing contests and don't worry about being rejected. The important thing is to try and to keep on trying."

As Sacramento's poet laureate, Knorr hopes to assemble a cadre of writers and go into classrooms to share their experiences but mainly to inspire young people to stay in touch with their creative sides. He's also making himself available as a speaker for corporate and nonprofit events through the auspices of the Sacramento Metropolitan Arts Commission, which selected him as poet laureate and serves as his booking agent (contact AAulenbacher@ cityofsacramento.org).

To give you an idea of Knorr's imagery and heart, I'm closing today's column with the closing of one of his poems, "Arriving at the Shore."

I've found myself at the kitchen table. The dog watches like I'm hiding in wheat. Across the room, she waits for me to spook. Outside, the shift of light and leaves. I will walk directionless a while arrive at one place to a small hand in mine, a drawing of a boat, a lake, a bear, and the fear pushed back behind the wonder of all new things.

Sept. 20, 2012

A film to remember by Matt Palmer

Matt Palmer is a graduate of Jesuit High School and the fabled New York University film school. He's 23 years old and dreams big: He hopes to enter his nearly completed documentary, "Friends of Mine," in the Sundance Film Festival four days from now. I think his movie may be too good for Sundance.

"Friends of Mine" follows two young men who become volunteer counselors at Camp ReCreation, a lakeside retreat in Susanville for children and adults with developmental disabilities such as Down Syndrome, Cerebral Palsy and autism. Palmer's film shows how Jordan Hamlin, a Jesuit High student, and Brian Gagliardi, a former student there and a recent graduate of UC Santa Barbara, begin their jobs with apprehension but grow to love their work and, more movingly, the campers.

"I fell in love with movies when I was 12 years old," Palmer tells me the other afternoon when he comes by my house and sets up a private screening of his film — on his computer, in my dining room. He apologizes for what isn't finished yet — color correcting, time-coding, the movie's music score. But while watching about 45 minutes of what will likely be a 90-minute movie, it's clear to me that he's put together a film that's both personal and universal. Without anyone making speeches about it on-screen, the film's theme seems to be not just tolerance of the disabled but also true acceptance.

At one point in the movie we hear young Hamlin lament that when he got to the camp, to earn his community service credits for school, he found it wasn't what he'd signed on for.

"I was 17 at the time," he says. "I could barely take care of myself. (Now I) have to take care of somebody else?"

If you'd like to see a promo for Palmer's film — and even better, contribute a few tax-deductible bucks to ensure its completion — head online to elsewherepictures.com.

And if you're wondering what film made young Palmer fall in love with movies, it was "Fargo," the morbidly funny Coen Brothers movie that made many of us reconsider the possible uses of wood-chippers. "Fargo" won a bunch of awards. But not at Sundance.

Oct. 22, 2012

New plot turn for novelist Kathryn Mattingly

El Dorado Hills-based author Kathryn Mattingly says that her new novel, "Benjamin" — which will be published in hardback and available in bookstores and online in May — "probably shares some traits" with her previous stories. "There's always a strong female heroine, a love triangle, everyone's trying to save a child and there's also a villain." (Sounds a little like a session of marriage counseling, doesn't it?)

But these are no bodice-ripping romance books, she's quick to clarify. "I write what's called literary fiction, for want of a better term," she says over coffee the other morning. "They're driven by character, not by plot. In popular fiction, authors decide what the action's going to be, then kind of drop their characters into it. I couldn't care less about that. I want to create my characters and then see what they're going to be up to." (Details about "Benjamin" are available from her Sacramento-based publisher, Winter Goose Publishing.)

Mattingly could be one of her own protagonists. A pretty, diminutive woman with pale blue eyes that also look green at certain angles, she's been a an award-winning professor, an editor, a writer, the mother of four children in their 30s and, for 41 years, a wife. She has a degree in art, which she's taught, but says she cut back on painting when she was a very young mom. "It was just awfully messy," she says. "I don't mean just the paint and brushes. I mean it takes all of your focus — and when you have four babies all demanding your attention, that's the definition of messy."

She laughs. "I mean, I already had two children before I even graduated from college."

Her husband, Dennis, is currently working as an arborist for a PG&E contractor. He previously worked in forest management and did marketing for a helicopter company before the economy went into its own tailspin. An athlete and outdoorsman, he sometimes accompanies his wife to writer conferences — and, while she's "sitting in a comfortable, air-conditioned room on a cruise ship," she says, "he heads off to participate in extreme sports." I'm guessing that dinner conversation has to be lively in the Mattingly household.

Though she was won Outstanding Teacher awards every year from 2007 to 2011 at the International Academy of Design & Technology — a private trade school with campuses in Natomas and other parts of the country — she was laid off more than a year ago when the institution decided to provide its general education courses online. Mattingly says she's still in touch with her colleagues at IADT and has "zero bad feelings about what happened." She smiles and raises her voice for the first and only time during our chat: "Which doesn't mean I'm not looking for a job!"

She holds the rather specialized degree, an MAT (master of arts, teaching), which is usually seen as a private-school credential. She's directed those — and their specialized programs — here and in the northwest.

Someone hire her before she sells "Benjamin" to a film producer — though either way, this story could have a very happy ending.

Fans and friends help entertainer Francie Dillon

Francie Dillon says she first noticed something had become different about her when she watched a video of one of her performances at a school assembly. "I noticed a kind of pulling on my lips," she says. "But instead of thinking there was something actually wrong, I just decided I needed to open my mouth more when I sang." Something was not only different, but also actually wrong. To date, nobody in the local medical community seems to know what that might be.

To mix metaphors, Dillon is a whirlpool of incandescence: an arts educator and children's entertainer whose voice and songs have been featured in Fairytale Town's "story-boxes" for years. Until the last two years, she was an athletic, deliberately over-scheduled performer. "I knew something started changing as much as two years ago, but I compensated," she says over coffee earlier this week. "In the middle of a song I'd start swaying back and forth and think, 'When did I become Stevie Wonder?' Then I noticed I was stomping one foot when playing the guitar and I thought, 'Oh, God, now I'm becoming Dolly Parton!' I guess I didn't want to notice anything — until my body forced me to."

Today, at 56, with her yet-to-be-diagnosed neurological condition, she uses what she calls "monkey arms" (forearm braces) to walk, has developed a stammer that seems to emerge mainly when she's overcome by emotion and will see her beloved Curtis Park home auctioned off Nov. 5 on the Sacramento County courthouse steps due to her having declared bankruptcy. "I take home $1,100 a month as a very part-time teacher at Sac State," she says. "Until this thing hit me, I was doing really well — I was entrepreneurial, I performed all over the region and I'd managed to provide for my daughters and myself." Now she's living in a rented studio apartment in East Sacramento ("They let me keep my dog and my cat," she says with a smile) and "thanking God for my benefits from CSUS."

Tomorrow evening at 5:30, Dillon's fans, friends and fellow musicians — including Mumbo Gumbo and the Jazz Report — are putting on a concert at Fairytale Town to raise money so she can have an emergency fund as she plunges into a concentrated search for an explanation, as well as some help on how to live with whatever she has. Tickets are available at the door at $20 per person or $50 per family. Capital Public Radio's Beth Ruyak — who had just interviewed Dillon for her "Insight" program before Dillon and I met for coffee — is the emcee.

Tomorrow, Dillon explains what it's like to be "Superman, suddenly surrounded by Kryptonite."

Nov. 2, 2012

"I feel like I'm Superman, suddenly surrounded by Kryptonite," says Francie Dillon, the multiple award-winning educator, singer and storyteller in explaining what it's like to find herself with an apparently neurological condition that renders her sometimes weak and sometimes stammering — and has yet to be diagnosed.

This evening at 5:30, a bazillion of her friends and fans, including Mumbo Gumbo and the Jazz Report, will hold a concert on her behalf at Fairytale Town, the Land Park children's venue whose electronic story-boxes — which feature Dillon's voice, songs and stories — have been delighting kids and their parents for well over a decade. The event ($25 per person or $50 per family at the door) was organized by local PR pro Terry Foley, whom I've written about in this space before (one of his sidelines these days is buying, creating and selling URLs). In his years with Borders Books, he frequently hired Dillon to perform at its area stores. Foley, who has brought Dillon to our interview (though she's still quite capable of driving), says, "She absolutely sparkles. I used to watch her sing and perform for the kids. I found myself completely enthralled. And as we know, I'm not a kid."

While I've heard Francie Dillon's work as a singer, songwriter and storyteller many times (I am, after all, a daddy), I never met her until she was given the award for Arts Educator of the Year at this year's "Prelude to the Season," the annual fundraising luncheon of the Arts & Business Council of Sacramento (I'm president its volunteer board). And while I realize this is a town known for giving standing ovations at the opening of envelopes, I can report that the one Dillon received here was one of the most heartfelt, teary-eyed salutes I've ever seen. Dillon almost missed it — she was paying attention to climbing down the stage steps after delivering a touching, hopeful and spontaneous acceptance speech, and didn't realize the audience was standing up for her. "Wasn't that something?" she says, her eyes misting and her voice growing husky.

Dillon has hazel eyes, an impish blonde hairdo and a solid, once-athletic body that she still propels heroically, using forearm braces. The "monkey arms," as she's chirpily dubbed them, were suggested to her by former Sacramento Mayor Heather Fargo, who was diagnosed with multiple sclerosis a few years ago. "Heather told me that there were two things to keep in mind when I came down with whatever this is," Dillon recalls: 'Keep your sense of humor and don't let your body define you.'"

That would extend to having others define your condition. Dillon says that a fellow she knows suggested her hair dye may be the cause of her problems. "I happened to let my hair go gray for a while because I retreated to my cave and didn't want to see anyone," she says. "And you know what? I didn't get better." She almost cackles at the memory. "Then I saw my reflection in a window as I (hobbled) by, gray hair, braces and all, and I said, 'I refuse to be that person.' So I dyed my hair back to blonde and crawled out of the cave."

Judith Horstman:
A tour guide for the brain

I f you're having trouble finding a holiday gift for those special people in your life who, as they grow older, fear that they're misplacing their marbles, I'd like to strongly recommend the newest book by Sacramento-based author Judith Horstman, "The Scientific American Healthy Aging Brain." Its subtitle is The Neuroscience of Making the Most of Your Mature Mind.

If you're wondering whom I'm referring to, gifting-wise, let me suggest myself as Exhibit A — a man who, as I've recounted here, recently located his long-missing cell phone in his refrigerator. In a six-pack carton of Stella Artois.

"Healthy Aging Brain" is Horstman's fourth effort for the Scientific American "brain series," hardcover books with enough charts, anecdotes and illustrations to make the journey a swift, lighthearted read. Its humor, warmth and accessibility are surprising only if you've never sat down over coffee with Horstman, a lively, energetic woman with playful you-can't-fool-me eyes peering over her stylish glasses. She moved to Sacramento County in 2003.

"I had a wonderful apartment in San Francisco but I wanted a garden," she says over a latte at Tupelo.

Unlike many "lay" science or tech writers, Horstman doesn't rely on third-party information providers — which is to say, she doesn't quote from articles about scientists but rather from articles by and interviews with the actual scientists (don't worry, she translates). In Journalism Land, this is called primary sourcing. It means Horstman doesn't extend her page count by engaging in random speculation or attempts to over-synthesize complex ideas. And, refreshingly, she never underestimates her readers, whom she takes by the figurative hand and leads on a never-boring journey into (and now I'm being literal) their own heads.

Among the gratifying findings in the book — which is available from amazon.com or by contacting Horstman via her website, judithhorstman.com — is a chart, very early on, called The Major Myths of Aging. A few snippets, which I've slightly re-punctuated:

"We used to think older people are unhappy. But now we know ... (that) people are actually happier in their 70s than at midlife."

"We used to think depression is part of growing old. But now we know (t)he depression rate among health elders is under 5 percent — less than half the U.S. average rate of 11.26 percent ..."

"We used to think that older people often regret their lives. But now we know (o)nly 1 percent of those over age 86 say their lives turned out worse than they expected."

Tomorrow, we pick a little more of Horstman's brain. Join us.

Dec. 18, 2012

We met author/journalist Judith Horstman in yesterday's column, whose most recent book, "The Scientific American Healthy Aging Brain" I thoroughly enjoyed reading. Or at least that's how my aging brain remembers the experience.

I'm not the only one who likes the book, though. Earlier this month, the Wall Street Journal featured it as one of the year's six best books on later life.

"This is, by far, the best time to be old in America," says Horstman, who lives in Sacramento and will be 73 in

February. She means it in terms of the progress medical science has made in understanding how the brain and body work together, and how some once-terminal illnesses can now be treated, "though not always," as chronic conditions. She scoffs at the long-held belief that human beings use only 10 percent of their brains. "False. We use all of it," she says flatly — even though I've told her about having misplaced my iPhone and seeing it turn up weeks later. In my refrigerator. In a six-pack carton of Stella Artois.

Horstman compiles a tidy living by writing her books and giving sought-after speeches around the world. In fact, she says she spends "at least a month a year out of the country." She's been freelancing full time since 1996 and says, "I write so that my 14-year-old grandson can understand it — and a neuroscientist will enjoy it."

Medical professionals are among her biggest fans. On the back cover of her new book, Dr. Mehmet Oz, whom I interviewed for the Business Journal in May, blurbs that Horstman "elegantly describes the well-aged brain and what the latest research suggests to preserve its power and its function." Dr. Marc Agronin, a geriatric psychiatrist and the author of the well-regarded book, "How We Age," calls Horstman's book "brilliant" and a "must-read."

Horstman's book is available from amazon.com and via her own website, judithhorstman.com. You can email her at the latter and receive a nice surprise: She actually replies. "I really like communicating with my readers," she says. Now there's a brainy idea.

Tony Ray Harvey
looks into dark corners

As a reporter, Tony Ray Harvey covers just about everything for the Sacramento Observer, the decades-old newspaper targeted to the region's African-American community — and, these days, distributed mainly through the area's churches.

As an author, he's been focused for eight years on a single, horrifying true-crime story that tore apart the Oak Park community in the 1980s: the killing of six young women, ages 16 to 29.

Harvey's book, "The Homicidal Handyman of Oak Park: Morris Solomon, Jr.," has just come out. It's compelling but because of the subject matter, unnerving. It's handsomely designed by Harvey himself but has some crime-scene photos you may not want to scrutinize while enjoying your morning bowl of steel-cut oatmeal.

"I want this to be a tool for the law enforcement community," Harvey told me the other morning at a coffee shop a few blocks from his newspaper's office on Alhambra Boulevard, just on the cusp of Oak Park. "I want cops to see that when people get killed in (under-served) communities, their murders should get the same attention as when it happens in affluent communities."

Harvey, who'll turn 48 next month, is wiry, intense and, given his obsession with grisly crimes, surprisingly good humored. Born in Champaign, Ill., he's lived and worked in Sacramento for nearly 25 years, first in the circulation department of the late Sacramento Union, and for the past 10 years as a reporter for the Observer.

210

He has nothing but praise for the cops who encouraged him to write his book and helped open doors to him — notably, former city of Sacramento homicide detective John Cabrera, who investigated both Morris Solomon Jr. and Dorothea Puente, the notorious boarding house operator in Alkali Flat who was convicted of murdering her tenants for their welfare checks (she died in prison nearly two years ago).

Harvey's book is available at the Avid Reader bookstore (15th and Broadway, the former site of Tower Books), or can be ordered online at authorhouse.com.

Tomorrow, we'll continue our chat with the author and hear about his own chats with Solomon, which took place on Death Row. Please join us — but not over breakfast.

Jan. 11, 2013

Tony Ray Harvey begins his book, "The Homicidal Handyman of Oak Park: Morris Solomon, Jr.," with an almost aerial view of Sacramento. He quotes from the Sacramento Convention & Visitors Bureau's 2007-08 visitor's guide ("Sacramento is known as the 'friendly city' — a good place to live, work and play.")

And he reminds us what longtime KXTV-TV Channel 10 news anchor Dick Cable said in a 1991 interview. "We've had some horrible crimes right around here," he told a reporter for the Sacramento Bee. "In the last five years since the Kings came to town, we've been talking about ourselves as an emerging world-class city. I don't know if the Kings have made us a world-class city, but it seems we're (right up) there for bizarre types of crimes."

Harvey then guides us through the region's past and gradually, but cleverly, eases in some fairly unfriendly reminders that we've had plenty of big-city, high-profile crimes occur here. (His book is available at the Avid Reader bookstore or online at authorhouse.com.)

"I'm totally into history," Harvey told me over coffee a few blocks from his office at the Sacramento Observer, where he's been reporting for the past decade.

As part of the research for his book, he managed to set up three interviews on San Quentin State Prison's Death Row with Solomon, the convicted murderer of six young women, who's supposedly been awaiting execution for 18 years.

"Oh, they're never going to execute him in this state," Harvey said dismissively. "He never confessed to the authorities and he never confessed to me when I talked to him." He says that Solomon, who was a drug addict — "Crack cocaine split the black community apart in the 1970s and '80s," he says — has gone from being a thin, shriveled presence into "a kind of tubby guy, being in prison all these years."

One of Harvey's sisters, Pennie Allen, is a sheriff's deputy in Champaign, Ill., his hometown. Another sister, Tammie Moore, works in the insurance business in Dayton, Ohio. He says his interest in writing and art originated was influenced by his mom, Rosa Guillory, "who always loved theatre. I saw a lot of movies growing up."

I'll wager that none of those was as gruesome as the real-life story he's become fixated on — and expertly draws us into in his disturbing, essential book.

GOOD INTENTIONS

HDTV comes with a dress code

I f you happened to tune into Channel Six's annual art auction this past weekend — specifically Saturday from 3-4 p.m. and Sunday from 4-5 — you have me at a disadvantage. You now know how dreadful I look on television while I still have no idea what you look like in sweatpants.

I went on camera at the request of KVIE's art curator, D. Oldham Neath, a longtime friend who's shown my paintings at her gallery, Archival Framing. My role was to discuss the artwork (as a longtime/small-time collector). I appeared with experienced media mavens Mary Jane Popp on Saturday and Jim Finnerty on Sunday. They did the actual auctioneering. I was what might be called the color commentator.

A few days earlier, the station had all of the hawkers and kibitzers come in so we could get familiar with the art as well as the studio. Signals got a little mixed. Apparently, the important thing was for us to relax. Have a conversation with the auctioneer. Be ourselves (in my case, a poor policy decision).

On the other hand, we were cautioned, remember: This is high-definition television. Every pore, every speck of spinach in our teeth, every nose hair, every wrinkle, and every bead of seat would be revealed in crystal detail.

Don't wear a checked shirt. Don't wear a striped tie (especially not with a checked shirt). Don't wear a black suit; if we did, since the studio's walls are black, we'd look like a bunch of disembodied heads overusing words like vibrancy, nuanced and fanciful.

It might not have looked like it but I turned out to be a very convincing art expert, at least to one person. I had said on the air on Saturday how much I admired the paintings of Gary Pruner (true) and how I had missed the chance to buy any at earlier auctions (also true). The bidding escalated.

When I got home, my wife Candy asked me if I'd really meant what I said about Pruner's work. Of course I did, I said. "Oh, good!" she said excitedly. "I'm the one who bought it!"

Good thing she looks so cute in sweatpants.

A restaurant with a mission

When my recent "clogs" about favorite places to have business lunches appeared, Michele Steeb wasted no time in inviting me to her favorite restaurant: Plates, which is operated by St. John's Shelter for Women & Children. Steeb just happens to be the organization's executive director.

First things first: the meal was terrific. I had pasta carbonara, one of the daily specials, and one of my favorites — for dinner, though, not for lunch. I'm not one of those people who can eat this luxuriously at lunch and still fit into their business suits (or front seats, for that matter).

Plates is located in the remodeled, still-cavernous commissary that served the U.S. Army Depot. It features a diverse menu (five different salads, five different sandwiches, "stove-top" entrées, satisfying side dishes — French or sweet potato fries, pasta or garden salads, fresh fruit — and house-made desserts. The restaurant's open for lunch from 11 a.m.-2 p.m. Monday-Friday, and is available for events "just about anytime."

I think this is a fine place for a business lunch, awards banquet or annual meeting because of the food and the site: just 10 minutes from downtown if you drive (rapidly) on Highway 50, take the Power Inn Road exit, head south to Fruitridge, turn left and then right at Business Park Drive. The signs will guide you in from there.

It's also soul nourishing. St. John's Shelter gives women and children from broken homes — and sometimes, more than broken, downright devastated — a chance to learn job and life skills. These women are your restaurant crew. "The idea is for women to gain and maintain employment," says

Steeb over a Chinese chicken salad that appeared larger than she is.

While the shelter's been around for 26 years, the restaurant opened on June 23, 2010. Steeb says it's on track to be profitable in the next six months.

I believe her. The former vice president of public affairs for the California Chamber of Commerce, she says that when her grandfather died, she felt moved to carry on his legacy of community activism. Joining the shelter's board of directors in 2006 — at a time when the phones were shut off for nonpayment of bills and "the shelter bounced two payroll checks" — she realized she'd found her calling. "I don't want to make this sound too dramatic," she says, "but I felt very 'led' to step in."

When Plates first opened, restaurateur Patrick Mulvaney spent two weeks donating his time as a mere-mortal line cook. In the time since, he and his wife Bobbin have donated hours, equipment and expertise to the enterprise. But what's even better than that? "The Mulvaneys have hired nine of our graduates," Steeb says. That certainly sits well.

Oct. 12, 2012

The man behind the blue trees

First there was John Guare's wonderful play "The House of Blue Leaves." Now, thanks to artist Konstantin Dimopoulos, Sacramento can boast of having The Street of Blue Trees.

By now you've probably heard the buzz about this art-cum-political project, on K Street between J and L. What you might not know is that Dimopoulos would like to do the same thing to a stretch of trees along the Amazon River.

I catch up with him the other amber-lit autumn morning as he and Ray Tretheway — former Sacramento city council member and full-time executive director of the Sacramento Tree Foundation — take a short break from coating the trunks of the trees in ultra-marine, a ravishing blue that Dimopoulos says Michelangelo concocted to paint the ceiling of the Sistine Chapel. (There were no Sherwin Williams stores back then, my research team assures me.)

Dimopoulos is a delightfully enthusiastic 55-year-old, with thick white hair, large, purposeful hands and, considering his name, an unexpected Australian accent. Reason for the latter: He comes from Greek parents, was born in Egypt but grew up in New Zealand. Because his wife and business manager, Adele, is Jewish, and because in that culture this means their four children are also Jewish, Dimopoulos grins and says, "So I'm Jewish, too."

The project, which the artist says is to draw attention to the deforestation happening around the globe, has been attracting a good deal of attention — but what I find the most enjoyable is that, with the exception of Sactown Magazine's participation, it's brought together sponsors not always celebrated for engaging in what might be called random acts of coolness. I'm talking about the Sacramento Convention & Visitors Bureau and the Sacramento Metropolitan Arts Commission, both of which are quasi-government agencies.

And then there's good ol' Ray Tretheway, a longtime and highly respected environmentalist. He is spattered with blue paint this brisk morning and, with the wide-eyed excitement of a 12-year-old boy, offers to take me up with him on an expandable painter's platform (necessary because the artist and his volunteers are painting the trunks from the ground up to 18-20 feet. "The leaves take over at that point, and we're not painting those," Dimopoulos says. "You have to leave something to the viewer's imagination").

Another project he's considering is painting purple spots along the streets of his hometown in Melbourne, Australia, and inscribing the names of local homeless people in them "to show that these are very real people and to encourage (more fortunate) people to either buy them a meal or give them a job. You can sometimes ignore the homeless but it's much more difficult to ignore someone named Bob," he says.

EDUCATORS AND
ARTS ORGANIZERS

Meet Sandra Kirschenmann

The energetic Sandra Kirschenmann becomes executive director of Drexel University's Sacramento Center for Graduate Studies on Dec. 12 — but first will fly to her apartment in Paris on Thanksgiving Day. She also owns a vineyard in Lodi. She is my new idol.

I caught up with Kirschenmann last Friday at Drexel's offices at One Capitol Mall in Old Sac. We spent the first 10 minutes discovering (a) we live a few blocks from each other — I've seen her walking her white Schnauzer and maybe her new black French bulldog ("I'm teaching him French," she says, a remark whose surrealism doesn't hit me until I'm back in the parking garage); (b) we were both widowed in the past few years; (c) we both know and think quite highly of Ann Madden Rice, CEO of the University of California Davis Medical Center (where Kirschenmann's late husband was treated for lymphoma); (d) we both love to cook (she's taught culinary arts but, unlike your feckless correspondent, looks too trim to have taken her work home with her).

Kirschenmann's friendly, arm-patting, how-ya-doin' manner is the polar opposite of the stereotypical college administrator or lifelong academic (she has almost as many degrees as those that separate Kevin Bacon from the rest of us, including a doctorate in education). A native Sacramentan, she attended Sacramento High School, the alma mater of Mayor Kevin Johnson, who concluded a laudatory statement about her being hired by Drexel with, "I'm especially proud that she's a fellow Dragon." You had to be there.

Among Kirschenmann's goals for Drexel, whose main campus is in Philadelphia, is to introduce an undergraduate

223

program into the school's currently all-graduate curriculum, though students would start at Drexel in their third year. "We have remarkable community colleges in this town to prepare people," she says. She ought to know. She attended Sac City and American River, earned her BA and MA degrees at University of California Davis, and her Ed.D. at Pacific, which we used to call UOP before it successfully rebranded itself.

Kirschenmann uses that word "remarkable" a lot. Having spent 32 years working for the Los Rios Community College District, most recently as its vice chancellor of resource development, she made the plunge into the private-school sector after researching Drexel's success stories (which she found "remarkable") and deciding that private schools "are a little more nimble than public schools. They take the full measure of their students: they look at students in depth, not just in terms of their education."

She's the daughter of a one-room schoolhouse teacher from South Dakota, now 93, and made it to the rank of lieutenant in the U.S. Army, where she learned to cook. She's also naturally competitive: she says that the MBA package at UCD costs a student $73,000 "unless there are scholarships," compared to Drexel's $58,000 — and "discounts are available," she says, particularly to veterans or those who hope to work in the nonprofit sector.

All in all, it sounds as though Drexel has made itself a remarkable hire.

Meet engineer-turned-producer Tom Huiskens

oncert producer Tom Huiskens, an engineer by training, learned the hard way that it's not easy being green. It had nothing to do with rain forests or sustainable construction. It was when he sang the part of Melchior, one of the magi visiting the Christ child in a production of Menotti's Amahl and the Night Visitors. Watching a video of the performance afterward, he realized that when he sang, "I sounded exactly like Kermit the Frog. No one had the heart to tell me."

At the invitation of concert promoter Valerie Weinberg (who sings jazz and pop as Valerie V), I sat down to lunch last week with Huiskens and his assistant, Michelle Bouvé — who used to work at KSSJ, the late and lamented "smooth jazz" station — at the Radisson, where Huiskens produces its jazz series. The final concert of 2011, commemorating the first 10 years of Huiskens' partnership with the hotel, will be "A Peter White Christmas" in the hotel's grand ballroom. Tickets are available online at huskyshows.com.

A powerfully built former college football player, Huiskens, 61, produced his first concert in 1992 while working for the late developer Fred Anderson of Rancho Murrieta and Pacific Coast Building Products fame. Anderson owned the fondly remembered Surge football team, which played at Sac State's renovated football stadium. Huiskens was in charge of that renovation when Anderson asked him to also book five non-football events for the season. "My first concert was Phil Collins and Genesis,"

Huiskens recalls, laughing at the memory. "I mean, I started out with the very best."

It hasn't exactly been downhill from there. Huiskens ended up producing shows — jazz, pop and all forms of rock — for Sleep Train Amphitheatre and Arco Arena (now Power Balance Pavilion, though maybe not for long if the company has to keep refunding customers for buying its signature panacea sports bracelet). He lives in Grass Valley, has three grown sons and is unavailable every Monday when he babysits his youngest of four grandkids, Barrett Lily, who's 15 months old.

One of Huiskens' more surprising gigs was a concert he produced for the group Fourplay on the driving range of Granite Bay Country Club. "We expected around 3,000 people," he says, "but 8,000 showed up." The Greyhound bus drivers who were supposed to shuttle the crowd from an orchard-turned-parking lot several blocks away — and back, which is significant to this story — decided to immediately go on strike during the concert since they weren't prepared, psychologically I guess, for this many passengers.

Huiskens ended up leading concertgoers back to their cars through an encirclement of buses after the show. "It was like Moses parting the Red Sea," he said — except some on the Exodus "were quite inebriated."

His most vivid memory of the night was when people started their cars simultaneously, turned on their headlights and "drove off in all directions" out of the orchard. "It was chaotic," Huiskens says. But, one guesses, still better than sounding like Kermit the Frog.

For Suzette Riddle, talk isn't cheap

"I think what I've been doing is nothing less than grieving," Suzette Riddle is telling me over coffee the other afternoon. She's mourning the closing of her brainchild, California Lectures.

Riddle started putting together the nonprofit organization 10 years ago, researching similar groups in Portland, Seattle, San Francisco and New York. She developed relationships with authors, agents and publishers, then spent the next eight years producing the speaker series.

For most of its run, California Lectures attracted sold-out audiences who came to hear Nobel and Pulitzer Prize winners in the ornate but surprisingly intimate main auditorium of the Crest Theatre in downtown Sacramento. Two of Riddle's most popular speakers, the late Norman Mailer and John Updike, gave their near-final talks here. David Sedaris, one of my faves, also spoke here — as did National Public Radio's essential Terry Gross and PBS's incomparable Jim Lehrer. (Personal note: Riddle had arranged for me to meet Lehrer when he was here in April of 2009. I wanted to thank him for helping me get through the first few months after my wife died two years before. He seemed puzzled and I explained that when I watched him deliver the news each evening in his calm, Midwestern voice, it reminded me that life really could go on. It choked him up. What a fine, fine man; no joke to follow.)

Riddle says the economy was the principal reason that California Lectures couldn't continue beyond 2011. Subscriptions and single-ticket sales had taken a nosedive, and contributed income — grants, donations and sponsorships — all but evaporated. "We tried to develop new

227

partnerships and I must have talked to more than a hundred people," she recalls. "No one wanted to see us go — but no one was in a position to give us the kind of help we needed."

The annual budget for California Lectures was around $260,000. The most Riddle paid for an author to come here to speak was $15,000, plus travel and hotel expenses. She won't say who got that much, and maintains that "all of our authors were a delight to work with."

Riddle herself is a delight: tallish, red-haired, green-eyed and a serious laugher, it's no surprise when she reveals she hails from Irish stock. At our first meeting to discuss the organization's closure, her eyes tear up intermittently; at our second get-together-I consulted with her as a member of Business Volunteers for the Arts, a program of the Arts & Business Council of Sacramento — she's already looking ahead.

"I'm exploring a number of opportunities," she says. "I have a lot of energy and creativity, and love to roll up my sleeves for an exciting project."

Put this woman to work! You can email her at suzriddle@earthlink.net

Tale of a transplanted Texan: My brother Jerry

Today's column, which runs a little longer than usual, isn't about a local businessperson, philanthropist or even Sacramento resident. It's about my brother, Jerry Goldman. This is his 71st birthday.

I realize that writing about a family member's birthday represents either the height or nadir of narcissism. I realize it but here we go.

When Jerry, a retired coach and teacher, flew here from Houston for my daughter's wedding last September, I kept previewing his arrival by telling people my "eldest brother, Jerry" would be attending the ceremony. "Eldest" implied I have more than one brother. But I no longer did. Our middle brother, Stuart, died several years ago, in his early 50s, after receiving a transfusion of gamma globulin. He contracted Hepatitis C, which morphed into cirrhosis, and died awaiting a liver transplant at Stanford University.

Both Jerry and I, separately, were close to Stu. For Jerry, Stu was his precocious, kid-genius younger brother. For me, Stu was the cynical, multi-talented older brother. His passing left Jerry, the eldest, and me, the youngest, to form our own alliance — which, owing to subsequent back-to-back tragedies, started as an initially tentative alliance and gradually strengthened into an immutable one.

Jerry and I are nine years and 10 months apart, a big age gap for siblings when they're young but not quite as ridiculous once you stumble into middle age. Our ages have been preceded by the same digit for only two months once each decade since I was 10 and he was 19 — which is to say, when I turned 20, he was 29 and 10 months old; when I turned 30, he was 39 and 10 months, and so on.

When we were kids in New York City's East Bronx section, Jerry was seriously into Western movies and Johnny Cash. Living in Texas for the past 30 years — and married to my wonderful sister-in-law, Joanie, a onetime horseback barrel racer — he's been able to immerse himself in a culture and sensibility thoroughly unlike the ones in which he grew up. He volunteers every year for the rodeo, for neighborhood watch and, lately, for search teams that look for missing persons. Those activities, combined with his teaching career, probably taught me more about social responsibility than any lecture or protest movement ever could.

We lived briefly in the small Southern California resort town of Lake Elsinore when we first moved to California in 1958. One day, my parents, grandparents and brother Stu left to attend the funeral of my father's kid sister, Lillian, who had died at the age of 33. Jerry stayed behind to babysit me. He took me to a movie then bought me a 10-gallon Stetson hat. I was not yet 8 years old and when it came time to hike back up a steep hill to the apartment where we were staying; he saw how tired I was and gave me a piggyback ride all the way home.

Happy birthday, bro'. May both of our rides continue.

Marilyn Hopkins:
A hunger for knowledge

S ome years ago, a series of books, albums, songs and comedy routines began with the phrase, "You don't have to be Jewish ..." What followed could be anything from "because when you're in love, the whole world is Jewish" or an advertisement on the order of "to love our bagels."

Touro University walks the talk, though. The Jewish-sponsored academic institution, which was founded 41 years ago and currently has about 19,000 students at various campuses, hired Marilyn Hopkins, a doctor of nursing science, to be provost and chief operating officer of its Vallejo campus in 2009. Hopkins, 63, who lives in Granite Bay, was raised as a Lutheran. And when she and her husband, Brian, a retired banker, attend church services, it's at Lutheran Church of the Resurrection in Placer County. In short, she hasn't converted.

She does, however, extol the virtues of kosher food. In fact, when she first started her job, "My goal was to jump right in and do great academic things. Instead, the first order of business was dealing with all of the complaints about the on-campus food. "I asked, 'What's wrong with it? Kosher food is great!' But no, it was pretty bad." So she and her staff found a chef who revamped the menu to not only make the orthodox Jewish fare tastier but also to satisfy the palates of her ethically diverse student body.

Touro University offers only graduate programs, in healthcare and education. The Vallejo campus (located, more precisely, on Mare Island) has roughly 1,500 students and

231

no dormitories. "One of the unfortunate outcomes of the economic downturn, but something that's been a plus for our students, is that there's affordable housing for rent and even to buy in the area," Hopkins says. (The City of Vallejo, as you'll recall, famously declared bankruptcy more than three years ago. "What's not as well known," says Hopkins, "is that the city worked its way out of bankruptcy last November.")

Just before taking her job at Touro, Hopkins was the dean of California State University Sacramento's College of Health and Human Services. She says that when he current contract with Touro expires later this year, "I'm sure I'll renew it for another three years." I ask her if living in Vallejo during the workweek and in Granite Bay on weekends takes its toll. "I do tend to spend more and more time at Touro," she admits. "But Granite Bay is where our family home is and where I'm still registered to vote." She grins almost mischievously. I'm not sure the mayor of Vallejo knows that."

Hopkins says that working in an environment dedicated to Jewish principles isn't that much of a stretch for her, even though she's half-Scandinavian and half-Italian. "The university's worldwide mission," she says without glancing at a single note-card, "is that education should be the key to personal inquiry, social justice, and service to society. You'll find that a lot of cultures and universities embrace that philosophy."

But do they love our bagels?

April 17, 2012

Ed Inch: Hard choices at Sac State

Ed Inch, dean of California State University Sacramento's College of Arts and Letters for the past eight eventful months, is a deceptively cheerful man. He's such a convivial lunch partner that it's easy to forget that this is a very serious, very determined and, of course, very well-read man. He's also considered, by present and former colleagues, to be a resourceful budgeter — a skill that's not only handy but also necessary as his bailiwick faces a 20 percent cutback now and the prospect of the university simply admitting no new students a year from now.

Over salads and flatbread at Piatti Ristorante, a durable flagship of Pavilions Shopping Center, I ask Inch, who's 52, if he's making sweeping cuts to reach that 20 percent goal. He frowns. "I'm not going to cut things across the board just so I can say I did it," he says. "When you do that, you cut some great programs along with programs that may need some extra nurturing. I'm not going to cripple the best things we do here."

Instead of doing any wholesale slashing, Inch has launched a number of initiatives that recognize "the areas in which we excel." Take music. "We've canceled two of our masters-of-music programs because they were under-performing. But we've hung onto the one that really works. And we separated our undergraduate music programs. One offers a very robust professional music degree for people who clearly will go out and make a living in the industry. That degree may require 150 or even 160 units, and may take five years to earn. The other's a more typical, but no less meaningful liberal-arts degree, a standard four-year

233

program, for people who enjoy studying the subject but aren't as likely to make music their livelihoods."

He's also reached into the business and arts community to form partnerships and, not coincidentally, to better brand his turf. "Do you realize the College of Arts and Letters puts on more than 200 events each year?" he asks. "Not all of these events are sold out, so I have empty seats." He chuckles as he says this, and before I have the chance to ask something brilliant like "This is a good thing?" he races on. "Those seats are free to me since they've already been budgeted for. That means I can use them to attract CEOs and local business leaders to events here. It allows me to work with community organizations, such as the Boys & Girls Clubs, to introduce kids to the arts, since they're sure not getting that in the public schools anymore.

"My goal," he continues, now with mock-menace, "is to hook 'em when they're young. If you connect with people early on in their formative years, they may just come back when they're ready for college."

Tomorrow, the professor opens up about his life. Let's call it Inch by Inch.

April 18, 2012

If things hadn't gone dicey in the commercial fishing industry back in the late 1980s, Ed Inch, dean of California State University Sacramento's College of Arts and Letters, might never have finished his doctorate.

"I thought sure I was going to spend the rest of my life working in fisheries," he says over lunch at Piatti Ristorante (see yesterday's clog for more from our discussion). He flew up to Alaska each summer to work there, simultaneously trying to write his dissertation. "But I was just too tired at the end of the day," he says. Being laid off turned out to be a great, if unintentional, career move: he earned his Ph.D. in speech communication from the University of Washington in 1992.

At the time of his hiring at Sac State last August, Inch had been a professor in the communication and theatre department at Pacific Lutheran University in Tacoma, Washington — but he was no stranger to Sac State, having served a year-long fellowship here in 2006-07, or to academic administration, having had a one-year gig as provost at Capital University in Columbus, Ohio.

While he doesn't use the specific term, Inch clearly considers himself a builder. His passion is bringing people of all ages into the university setting — and expanding that setting into the region. "We're in a community that, in some ways, embraces 'small' more than large," he says. "Small art galleries, small businesses, locally owned restaurants. Our job is to (facilitate) mutual access."

As an example, Inch points to the prospect of having multilingual students serve as docents when young people and adults "from all cultures" visit the campus. "They can take people who haven't been exposed to visual art — or who've been intimidated by it — into our art classes and galleries and indicate the kind of themes they might want to look for. The same can be done in all of our programs. The most important thing for me in bringing people together is to create a common experience for them to share. Once you create that moment, you can build on it."

Inch says he'd like to resurrect a currently unfunded certificate program in arts leadership "for students who'd like to devote their lives and careers to what I call the cultural industries. The fact is, most people aren't going to make a living in the arts, as artists — but there's no reason why they can't be connected to them, all of their lives."

You might expect a fellow like Ed Inch to be a collector of rare books or out-of-print record albums — in short, scholarly ephemera. But he's a bit more of an action figure than that: he has a collection of vintage cameras "from the 1920s, '30s and '40s that my grandfather bought and used. I want to start using them again, too. There's so much to see and capture, just in Sacramento."

Who knows? Maybe he'll even photograph some fisheries.

Julie Hirota:
Engineering art from fabric

In two months, Julie Hirota will mark her second year at the CEO of Roseville's Blue Line Gallery, one of the region's most innovative showcases for long-established and up-and-coming artists. Not bad for a mechanical engineer.

I'm sitting with Hirota in her chocolate-walled, smallish office at the gallery (rosevillearts.org), which is on the ground floor of a city parking garage, next door to the town's historic Tower Theater. In the first few minutes of our chat, Hirota is interrupted three times by buzzes and beeps from her staff. "I guess there's no real point in my having a door here," she says dryly.

I say I don't mind if she has to take a call. After all, she has two young children (Gracie, who's 10, and Ben, who's seven); a highly respected artist/curator (Tony Natsoulas, whose vision has been guiding the gallery's current show, "Plates, Totems & Teapots"); and a board of directors, any or all of whom may need to reach her. "I have a feeling it's one of my staff asking, 'Where's the credit card?'" she says. "Believe me, if it was important, they'd think nothing of popping in."

Before joining Blue Line Gallery, first as its development director, the New York native worked as a mechanical engineer in the Roseville offices of NEC (now owned by the German electronics firm Telefunken) and Hewlett-Packard. Hirota had started seeing her husband, Aaron, an engineering manager, when they were students at UC Davis. She says the desire "to really make art" first seized her when she was expecting their first child and was lining up her life as a stay-at-home mom. She began designing and producing quilts that soon were being featured in shows in big-ticket art-loving cities such as La Jolla and San Francisco. She even wrote a how-to book on the process: "Art Glass Quilts: New Subtractive Appliqué Technique," an e-book.

"The quilting industry is its own little niche market," she says. "As I watched the economy collapse a few years ago, as an artist I saw a lot of morale collapse, too, especially mine. I think the turning point for me-to get back into the job market-came when I was a way on a three-day trip to sell my quilts. I ended up missing my daughter's swim meet and, naturally, it was the one where she posted her best time ever. And I didn't sell anything on the trip!"

These days, Hirota continues to volunteer at her kids' schools and to travel the region to spread the word about Blue Line, which as a nonprofit organization is one of the few galleries where a portion of your purchase may be tax-deductible.

She also remains a working artist. In fact, she created a clever ceramic serving dish for Blue Line's current show. Its title: "Too Many Things on My Plate."

Elliott Fouts is back

I f you're in town this weekend by yourself or want to dazzle your house guests, pop on over to Elliott Fouts' new art gallery at 1831 P St. in midtown Sacramento. The first show features Chris Stott's iconic (and possibly ironic) paintings of day-to-day objects.

This is Fouts' third gallery. He had one in Granite Bay for five years and, more recently, on J Street in East Sacramento, where he became a neighborhood fixture for seven years. "I've been lucky that my demographic has followed me around pretty much," he says. "When I was in Granite Bay — actually, just one block out of Roseville — half of my clients were coming from Sacramento. People here buy art. I mean, there are something like 20 galleries in town."

The new gallery is 5,600 square feet, twice the size of his now-closed J Street gallery. "What I like even more than the increase in exhibit space," he says, "is that the rooms are wider. You can actually step back and look at the art."

Fouts is 57 years old and appears boyish except for his graying hair and the sardonic look that takes over his face when suffering fools (and yes, he's shown it to me and I know the implications of that). He says he hits the road "fairly often" to sell his artists' work, or prints of them, to other galleries throughout California, admitting he's "not much of a closer" as a salesman but says he makes up for it with "attention and humor. People like self-deprecating people — and I have a lot to deprecate myself about."

This time out, Fouts owns the building, the former location of Fantasia Jewelers. He says he designed the space but gives ample credit to the architect who translated his vision, Dennis Greenbaum; to Marc Foster, the sculptor who designed the very cool sliding walls that hide or display frame samples; and to his hard-working contractor, Ken Dyer. The gallery has a parking lot and a kitchen, both of which allow Fouts to rent out or lend the space for fundraisers. The Sacramento Philharmonic will hold an event here in June and the Center for Contemporary Art will host one in November.

Since the space sat vacant for about four years, I ask if there were special problems in gutting and renovating it. "I didn't find any vermin of any kind," he says, offering me what I recognize as a sardonic look.

Orchestra backer Gus Guichard looks ahead

L istening to Gus Guichard's melodious and mellifluous voice, I tell him I find it hard to believe that this longtime board member of the 49-year-old Camellia Symphony Orchestra is not himself a musician. "Well, I listen very well," he says with a wry smile.

Guichard is 81, has the physique and wits of a much younger man and is looking forward to two milestone events in the next few weeks. The first is the orchestra's major fundraiser, "A Black & White Affair," a food, wine and music event this Sunday from 4:30 to 7:30 p.m. at Scribner Bend Vineyard in the Delta town of Clarksburg. Tickets and other information are online at camelliasymphony.org.

The second milestone is likely to occur on July 1, when the orchestra, familiarly referred to as the CSO, begins its new fiscal (and 50th) year. That's also when Guichard will rejoin the board he's been on for a total of 11 years. "We have a stupid bylaw," he explains, seeming to fight off a chuckle, "that says after you've been on the board for five years, you have to go off it for at least a year. I like to call the past year my sabbatical — though people called me often enough during it that I never really felt I left."

Guichard (it's pronounced "gish-ARD") retired more than a decade ago as the human resources vice chancellor of California Community Colleges, the largest higher-education system in the country. "For one 12-month period (in the 1980s), I even served as acting chancellor," he says. His enthusiasm for the state's community colleges is infectious. "I just love this system," he says. "It gives people, who might never have had it, a chance to get a solid education." Before going into administration, Guichard taught art history at Santa Rosa Junior College for six years. The subject area remains "a major passion" of his, as does music.

"I enjoy many forms and genres of music," he says, "but if I were pushed into saying what I like the most it would be early Baroque, such as Bach and Scarlatti." His taste in visual art runs toward pre-Baroque painters — and, citing Michelangelo Merisi da Caravaggio as a personal favorite, recounts that on one of his several trips to Europe since retiring, he sought our four churches in Rome that displayed his work. "We knew that each of the churches had coin-operated lights to illuminate the work," he says, "so we were sure to bring along many coins."

Guichard was born in New Orleans (no surprise when you hear him pronounce it "NOR-lins"). He grew up, he says, surrounded by "an extended family that had a lot of expectations for me. They said, 'You will be good at whatever the hell you do in life.' It motivated me."

I hope to see you at Sunday's fundraiser for the Camellia Symphony. It ought to be a fine opportunity to listen very well.

An extraordinary professor: Albert Yee

A lbert Yee is one of those college teachers you remember the rest of your life. You realize, sometimes years later, that when this guy was showing up in class dressed in an Angry Birds T-shirt or impersonating Marlon Brando as "The Godfather," you were simultaneously learning not only math and science but also real-life skills — like "how credit card debt works and why waiting to win the lottery doesn't constitute retirement planning."

Yee is the first full-time math and science professor at William Jessup University, the faith-based college whose sprawling Rocklin campus was once a Herman Miller manufacturing plant. He has also become, in just one year of full-time teaching, one of the university's more popular professors.

"I have 40 students in one of my classes, which made me write a 'memo to self' to start capping enrollment," he tells me yesterday over coffee at Tower Café. "Caffeinate me!" he cheerfully tells the waitress when he goes for his second cup.

It's not as though he needs the adrenaline boost. At 46, Yee is an avid fencer and bicyclist who often drives from his Davis home to south Roseville, where he removes his fold-up bike and pedals the rest of the way to work. He also knows what grips him and what doesn't: he originally thought of a full-time career in physics (he was named for Albert Einstein) but eventually came to feel that the field "was starting to sound like something out of Dr. Seuss, with up-quarks, down-quarks, spin and other whimsical terminology."

He holds a Ph.D. in mechanical engineering from UC Berkeley but earned both his masters and bachelors at Cal's legendary football rival, Stanford University. "You don't want to be in our home on the day of the big game," he says.

Among the math classes Yee teaches is a general education-required course in analytical inquiry. "I tell the students to forget about that name," he says, "and instead think of it under this title: 'The One Math Class You Need to Take To Graduate.'"

Tomorrow: For Dr. Yee, "God rocks!"

Aug. 1, 2012

I'm asking the real-life but highly animated Albert Yee, the first full-time math and science professor at faith-based William Jessup University, if he ever feels conflicted about being a mechanical engineer/mathematician in a Christian academic environment, since most of us have the (perhaps stereotypical) idea that when it comes to science and God, never the twain shall meet.

"That's always portrayed as a conflict," he says. "The notion is that if you're a scientist, you can't be a person of faith — and that if you're a person of faith, you think of scientists as being evil pagans.

"I think it's all pretty silly," he continues. "It's your world view that affects how you view science — but science stays exactly the same. It's like picking up a hammer and saying, 'This is a Muslim hammer' or 'This is a Christian hammer.' Well, get over it: it's just a hammer! And for me, as a scientist, God rocks!"

This is Yee's first teaching position. He worked as a mechanical engineer for many years (he's 46) where he was involved in creating robotics and medical devices. Now he's creating a department at Jessup. "My goal is to put myself out of a job at some point," he says, "by hiring enough great teachers and department heads. My dream is to start an engineering department here, though I always want to teach. Nothing has ever gripped me quite like teaching. It's the hardest job I've ever loved."

Yee's wife of 21 years, Angela, is a pastor at Universal Covenant Church in Davis. She started out as a graphic designer — and that, Yee says, caused some concern at home when he was dating her. "In my family, you need a 'D' after your name, whether it's an M.D., Ph.D. or Ed.D.," he says. Yee's father, Kane, was a professor of mathematics at Kansas State University, but started out in a "dirt-poor village" working on the family's farm in the Toisan area of southern China ("He spent the day hunting for eels with his toes.") His mother, Maxine, is a computer scientist. His sister, Audrey Westfall, is a neurologist. Yes, that's a lot of "D"s.

The couple's children have the potential to be overachievers, too. Son Daniel, 17, is about to study managerial economics at UC Davis "but his real dream is to conquer the world," Yee says. Daughter Megan, 15, wants to be a film director and cinematographer and has already produced a spy satire that garners some satisfying hits on YouTube.

I ask Yee if, looking back, he could say that his career path, through physics, math and science, was always apparent. "I'm not sure," he says with a broad smile. "If it helps, you can say that I started out by playing with Legos."

Sacramento's musical man: Richard Lewis

Richard Lewis strolls to the table I've just grabbed at Lucca Restaurant, on J at 16th Street, and explains that because his office is a block away, "I schedule most of my lunch meetings here and, naturally, am always late." He isn't (I'm early). He wears an untucked short-sleeve Mazatlan-style shirt, shorts and sandals, still manages to look impeccable. "I just take my pills and do as I'm told," he says in the strong voice and wry tone that have always made him a kick to hang with.

Lewis is the executive producer, president and CEO of California Musical Theatre, which includes three professional venues: the Music Circus, Broadway Sacramento and Cosmopolitan Cabaret.

Each summer, the Music Circus produces and presents tried-and-true musicals, the kind that have you humming the tunes as you enter the theatre — which, for decades, was a huge tent pitched on the corner of 15th and G Streets and is now a permanent playhouse-in-the-round at the same location. Broadway Sacramento, which sounds as though it's going to consist of talented local kids singing their hearts out while dreaming of making it to the Great White Way, is actually a presenting theater: it brings national touring companies of newer works, almost always musicals, to the Sacramento Community Center Theater.

The Cosmopolitan Cabaret, which Lewis says "has yet to find the perfect formula," has morphed into a supper club that imports or home-grows top-quality singers and comics in themed shows (such as "My Way," an enjoyable tribute to the songs made famous by Frank Sinatra, presented a couple of years ago). Its current offering is "Triple Espresso," a satirical revue.

I ask Lewis if CMT was hard-hit by the economic recession and he prefaces his remarks with a Dean Martin-like, "Ohhhhh, yeah!"

"We lost significant amounts of money three or four years in a row," he says. "We went from providing our employees with a 10 percent pension plan which is now down to around 0.5 percent. We had pay cuts followed by pay cuts followed by layoffs followed by pay cuts. We did a reduction in force — don't you hate that term? — with our administrative staff, reducing it by about 25 percent. My own benefits package is down 50 percent."

He remains optimistic and positively buoyant about what comes next, however. "We're doing more with less," he says. "The trouble is, we've been doing it so long we can now do anything with nothing." When I laugh he is quick to credit the remark: "Greg Smith, executive director of the Sacramento Ballet, said that."

Monday: A big, beloved show returns to Sacramento — which Lewis says he's allowed to "reveal but not announce."

Aug. 27, 2012

Richard Lewis runs California Musical Theatre and was the driving force to build the permanent home for its beloved Music Circus, the once-tented playhouse-in-the round which, as I indicated last week, plays it pretty safe on the musicals it presents (one walks in humming the tunes). I ask him over lunch if CMT's demographic has changed much since it was first co-founded by his dad in the early 1950s. "Not really," he says, his body language (leaning forward and widening his eyes) telegraphing the subsequent quip. "There's a 50-year-old born every minute. Chris McSwain once said that."

McSwain, a former marketing pro for CMT, is now business manager for Old Sacramento. I point this out because I respect McSwain but, more to the point, think it demonstrates Lewis's generosity in crediting others.

If you haven't heard the news, which was scheduled to be officially announced today, CMT is bringing "Le Mis" back to Sacramento on May 29, 2013. Actually, "announced" isn't quite the right word. "The producers of the show didn't want me to 'announce' it was coming to Sacramento until it closed in San Francisco (yesterday). I could 'reveal' it but not 'announce' it. They're afraid that if I 'announced' it prematurely, people would stay away from seeing the show in that little suburb down I-80 called San Francisco and instead flock to see the show in the metropolis we call Sacramento."

Lewis manages all of those quotation marks with his voice. And he almost never follows jokes like these with a smile, mainly because he seems to be smiling the entire time he's talking to you — a little like a friendlier version of Batman's nemesis, The Joker. As a result, you listen and watch a little more carefully to discern when he's kidding, and when he's not.

In truth, he's a very serious man: a husband and father, a businessperson and the heir of a show-biz dynasty. He's also a secret iconoclast — a former Disneyland employee who faced disciplinary action in 1980 because he wore, and still wears, a small earring in his right ear. "Disney has the Disney Look Book for people who work in the park and it says that earrings may be worn if they're less than a quarter-inch in diameter," he says. "I pointed out that mine is. They meant what women could wear. But they didn't say that."

Lewis looks 40 but turns 60 on Nov. 12 and plans to be in Florence, with his wife Joann. "I don't like parties and I particularly don't like surprise parties," he says. Bet he'd know how to stage a really good one.

Meet fundraiser Steve Weiss

I f it were in his nature to do so, Steve Weiss could just name-drop for a living. But he's not like that.

The owner and founder of The Weiss Group, based in downtown Sacramento, is a strategic marketing consultant who also devotes a fair amount of his workweek to running management meetings and retreats for companies and nonprofits. (The term-of-art is "facilitating," but that always sounds to me as if someone is in the process of becoming a building. I believe this is referred to as having an edifice complex.)

Weiss, who's 48, is an experienced fundraiser who helped pave the way for the Mondavi Center for the Performing Arts to become a reality. He's also a public relations pro and all-around "mensch" — a Yiddish word that means "person" but is used to evoke more than that, in the way that being humane is considered a notch up from being all-too-human.

As he sips hot tea one recent afternoon, at my insistence he recounts some of the boldface names he either met or spent a good deal of time with during his days working at UC Davis Presents, the popular lecture series: former Pres. Jimmy Carter, Bishop Desmond Tutu, cellist Yo-Yo Ma, the late politician Jack Kemp, author Alice Walker, and former California Assemblyman Tom Hayden. "Tom had asked, 'Would you mind if I bring my wife?'" Weiss recalls. "Seeing as how it was Jane Fonda, I said, 'I guess that'll be OK.'" He grins mischievously.

On Weiss's watch, the legendary folksinger Joan Baez trilled "Amazing Grace" a cappella in the quad at the University of California Davis. "It was a moment I'll never forget," Weiss says, "and neither will anyone who came to hear her or just happened to be walking by and probably thought, 'Hey, that sounds like a pretty good singer, I ought to go by and listen.' That's exactly what I wanted to happen."

Weiss helped UCD raise $10 million, then philanthropist Barbara Jackson donated another $5 million, to make the Mondavi Center a reality — and bear in mind this was before the late Robert Mondavi even became involved and gave the place its name. When it looked as though the center would be built, UCD's chancellor at the time, Larry Vanderhoef, asked Weiss to stay on the job and manage the place.

"I told him how flattered I was," Weiss says. "But the problem was, I didn't want to run a building. I wanted to build a building."

On Monday, Weiss talks about what can and should happen at an organization's retreat. It's not about the doughnuts.

Feb. 11, 2013

Since you didn't ask, my view of management retreats — as expressed in "Memos from Hell," the opening chapter of my first book — can be summarized thus: After spending a grueling workweek with people you don't necessarily like, you get to spend your weekend doing the same thing, only now while wearing a flannel shirt.

Steve Weiss, who helps prepare and facilitate retreats as one of his firm's activities, generously laughs at my observation — then pretty much laughs it off. "Retreats can be great for inspiring candor and real planning," he says. "The key is to do the advance work and keep things on an even keel. The important thing for a retreat's organizers, and for me, is to frame the conversation from the outset, as in 'Here's what we hope to accomplish today' — and then, allowing genuine conversations to happen."

Weiss says he spends time before a retreat with the organization's key staff. He also does independent research on the group. "There's nothing worse than my showing up and not having a sense of a company's or (volunteer) board's history," he says. "It's not only insulting. It's completely non-productive. I often follow up with the leaders afterward, too."

Since retreat participants frequently have questions they want to ask of their bosses but feel intimidated about doing so in front of them, Weiss has everyone write down questions and give them to him. He then shuffles the note cards or paper scraps and redistributes them so that each question gets asked — but not by the person who initially wrote it. "I ask a lot of questions the staff won't ask, regardless of the anonymity," he says. "I'm fairly intuitive and inquisitive by nature, so no one sees me as advocating for anything except honesty."

After Weiss graduated from University of California Davis with a degree in agricultural and managerial economics, he stayed on to work there, eventually becoming director of University Cultural Programs and helping organize the multi-million-dollar capital campaign that eventually funded the construction of the Mondavi Center for the Performing Arts. As we learned in Friday's column, Weiss was offered the job to stay at UCD and run the center. Instead, he accepted a post in 1998 with the Sacramento Bee. He ended up staying there nine years, eventually becoming the paper's vice president for marketing and public affairs, overseeing a staff of 20.

"I left the Bee on November 30 of 2007 and had the website to my new business up and running on December 1, 2007," he says. "I always wanted to own my own business and you might say I was ready for it."

While he keeps his office-for-one in downtown Sacramento — he works with "a group of reliable subcontractors, when needed" — Weiss lives in Davis with his wife Andrea, who also owns her own business (she's a career counselor) and their three sons: Jacob, 19; Sam, 16; and Eli, 13. Along the way Weiss has been deeply involved with charities and nonprofits, most notably as chairman of the KVIE-TV volunteer board of directors, and taught a class in business organization for three years at his alma mater. "I think I learned more than the kids did," he says.

Spoken like a true facilitator.

OF MEDIA AND MARKETING

Answers to questions you haven't asked

In the past few years, I've written copy for about 50 websites for my marketing and public relations clients, but never created one for my own work. I'm changing that in the next several weeks, mainly because I've finally come up with a list of NAQs (Never Asked Questions) for my site:

Q: How do you manage to write this column five days a week? Do you have any tips for bloggers?

A: I sure do. My secret is to reuse as many words as possible. My favorites are "the," "whom" and "oddly enough." This cuts down on my research and writing time; naturally, I pass the savings on to you.

Q: Do you receive your morning news in print or on a tablet?

A: Actually, I receive it in print; then, to get through the day, I take two tablets.

Q: Since your column/blog ("clog") occasionally gets political, how are you handicapping the presidential election?

A: I'm not. The candidates will do that.

Q: As a follow-up question: Do you ever plan in advance what you're going to say?

A: I've been married three times. Apparently not.

Q: My niece is considering a career in newspapers. What
would you recommend?

A: Why should she limit herself to newspapers? Why not
open a typewriter repair shop or sell VHS tapes door-
to-door?

Q: Briefs or boxers?

A: I prefer subpoenas and tabbies.

Q: From the look of the tiny photo they run of you with
your column, I keep wondering if it's actually a life-
size portrait. I'll take my answer off the air.

A: I'd like to answer that in detail but my arms hurt from
trying to reach the keyboard and my feet from trying
to reach the ground. Making matters worse, my tabby
just walked into my office.

A gathering of broadcast legends

I had a charming, nostalgic time last Thursday speaking at a luncheon held by Valley Broadcasting Legends. As you can imagine, this is a group of mainly retired news media guys, many of whom remain recognizable but only one of whom views himself as legendary. (My lips are sealed as to whom that might be. After all, I hope to get invited back someday. It's one of the few places someone my age can go and be called "Kid.")

I'd been asked a few months ago by a pal, meteorologist Kristine Hanson, to talk to the group. Back then, I was going to be on a panel with the Sacramento Bee's Dan Walters and Marcos Breton, both of whom I admire, talking about the presidential election. We were going to convene at the Buggy Whip restaurant.

By the time the day came around, however, the venue had been shifted to Club Pheasant in West Sacramento, Walters and Breton were nowhere in evidence, owing to other commitments, and both Kevin Riggs and I were supposed to deliver actual speeches, not just make snarky, ad-libbed panel comments, one after the other. For all I know, Hanson (who at the last minute was also unable to attend) had also predicted a twister to descend on West Sac that day.

Riggs is a former anchor for Channel 3, now a partner in Randall Communications, and one of the more effortlessly polished speakers I've ever had the misfortune to follow to a lectern. Since he's a political consultant, he had brought a truckload of those items I rarely use (facts) and has the kind of deep, modulated voice that would reassure you even if he were discussing that World War III had just been declared.

259

Since I had prepared nothing but coffee that day, I decided that the best thing to do was piggyback on Riggs' comments. Asked whether that evening's vice presidential candidate debate would likely change the face of the election, he said he didn't think so. That allowed me to say, when I lumbered to the dais, "I don't agree with Kevin at all — as I was just saying to Vice President Lloyd Bentsen the other day."

For those of you too young to remember, the late Sen. Bentsen debated Sen. Dan Quayle in one such V-P candidate debate, in 1988. It was made memorable by Bentsen's very rehearsed but indelible putdown, "Senator, you're no Jack Kennedy." (Quayle had been comparing himself to JFK, though not nearly as obnoxiously as Bentsen's comment made it sound.) Now, if you're still too young to remember — I would think reading this paragraph is aging you — Quayle, that year's Sarah Palin, went on to become Vice President of the United States.

Anyway, it got a great laugh. At least I think it was laughter. Considering the average age of the attendees, I suppose it could have been 50 defibrillators shorting out at once. That would surely be the stuff of legends.

Jan. 7, 2013

This is off the record

During the recent phony-baloney brinkmanship to strike a federal budget deal, there were a number of news stories in which anonymous sources were quoted. The justification for their namelessness usually went something like this: "One well-placed source, who spoke on condition of anonymity because he hadn't been authorized to comment on the negotiations, said —"

In other words, a so-called authority hadn't been authorized to speak by the authorities.

I don't know how you feel about it, but when I read unattributed remarks it makes me irritable for a couple of reasons. First, if it happens to be a local story, it annoys me that I can't figure out who the leak was (since I know many of them and occasionally rely on them for story tips — but never quotes). Second, why are some individuals so absurdly scared of being quoted by name if they really are in a position to know what they're talking about?

In the early 1980s, when I was the official spokesman for the UC Davis Medical Center during a period of crisis — far worse than the controversy now in play, though the current one may still yield some more developments — a now-retired reporter for a still-active local newspaper called to ask me a bunch of questions about what was going on at the teaching hospital. To be sure, I measured my words as carefully as I could — but I was candid about the problems and what was being done to resolve them. The reporter excitedly asked, maybe three times during our 10-minute chat, if my comments were "for the record" and "for attribution." I said yes to both.

The story appeared the next day but my name didn't. I had become a "reliable source" at UCDMC. I called the reporter and asked why he didn't quote me by name. He said — and here, I must quote him — that the way he did it "it was more dramatic." True story.

Here's another. A few years ago, I was having a drink with a veteran reporter, now deceased, and asked him about his notable ability to find people to comment, even anonymously, on sometimes scandalous issues. "Oh," he said, laughing and indisputably marinated, "I usually just make them up." I laughed, too — then realized he was serious. I asked, "Do you make up the sources or the quotes?" "Same thing," he said.

I'd tell you who this fellow was but I think he'd have preferred I quote him on condition of anonymity — due, of course, to his condition of non-sobriety.

COMMUNITY MEMBERS
AND LEADERS

Downtown Sacramento resident Emily Gerber

E mily Gerber is 30 years old, works "about .53 miles" from her apartment in downtown Sacramento and loves the area. And yet: "I'm starting to think it's better to save up all my shopping and go to Roseville once a month, where I can park as long as I'd like," she says.

If that sounds like urban heresy, you should hear her out, as I do late one afternoon to get the perspective of a downtown resident about the city's core. We're at a table in The Grange, the iconic restaurant on the ground floor of the splendid Citizens Hotel at 10th and I Streets, over a vodka martini and non-alcoholic spritzer (spoiler alert: Gerber is sipping the spritzer). Gerber has walked here after getting off work from her job as an associate governmental program analyst (this means she staffs the information technology help desk) at the state Dept. of Developmental Services. Her office is in a building at 9th and P Streets and she lives at 8th and J Streets. Her daily commute is almost like working at home. Even so, she hates, hates, hates the parking situation in the heart of the city.

"Have you ever tried to drive to lunch around here?" she asks, not the least bit rhetorically. "You pull up to a restaurant and there's only one-hour parking, which means you either have to interrupt your lunch to go out and re-park your car or get a ticket that's, like, $50. This is what's killing downtown."

Gerber, a Sacramento native, also thinks the K Street Mall can be greatly improved (who doesn't?). But she's not talking about the usual suggestions, which have ranged from reopening it to traffic (which has been done, with mixed results to date) to exploding nuclear devices from 7th to 12th Streets (which I really can't recommend).

"Why do people who live downtown have to drive to go get their groceries," she says, "when they could put a Trader Joe's or a similar store on K Street?" When I suggest that the Safeway store at 1814 19th St. would be a pretty easy walk for her, and she could tote her bags back in a foldable cart, she says, "Well, I already do that. But it's summer now. If you schlep a carton of ice cream home it'll melt."

Tomorrow: Some helpful hints from Emily.

July 17, 2012

"I think I missed my calling. I should have been an urban planner," Emily Gerber says. Then she adds, "I'm bossy," as though that further qualifies her for the job.

Gerber, a 30-year-old resident and state employee in downtown Sacramento, would like to see St. Rose of Lima Park, the site of an annual ice skating rink on K Street, converted into "a permanent farmer's market, covered, so people could go to it regardless of the weather." She'd also enjoy having a small grocery store at 7th and K Streets, as well as a "boutique-y kind of clothing store."

Gerber says she's a fan of the Ferry Building near San Francisco's Bay Bridge and doesn't see why its basic business model — dozens of stores and eateries packed into one structure — couldn't be duplicated here. When I tell her I used to own a condo up the hill from the Ferry Building until a couple of years ago, she reacts excitedly, as though I've told her that one of my close friends is a movie star.

We're having an after-work chat at The Grange, the restaurant in the Citizens Hotel, where Gerber is giving me an ordinary city-dweller's perspective on downtown. She's walked over from her office at 9th and P Streets and, when we're done with our chat, she'll walk to her apartment at 8th and J. Pretty convenient.

"I love walking to work," she says. "I love being able to come home, put on some dressier shoes and walking to dinner. I love the energy of downtown. It's not pretty in a conventional sense. It's not like going to Tahoe or looking at a beautiful garden, but I like it."

What she doesn't like, as she made clear in yesterday's column, is the parking situation. She despises the one-hour parking limits, especially near restaurants and stores, and thinks the city should develop a parking pass, like a debit card, that could be loaded up with hours and renewable once you'd parked up to your limit.

Gerber doesn't like the fact that the most ubiquitous retail outlets downtown are saloons. "When I think of my overall vision (for the future) of Sacramento, it just doesn't include bar after bar after bar." She'd like to see a few more live music venues ("I'm a jazz fan") and parks, such as Cesar Chavez Plaza — which is between Sacramento city hall and where we're chatting — "that I could walk my dog in without constantly looking over my shoulder."

That dog, by the way, is a Golden Retriever named Sam. They live together in a small studio apartment at the Lofts on J development. Gerber plays the cello, which probably takes up as much space as Sam. She also has a thoroughbred horse named Lizzie. "She's retired," Gerber says. I hope Lizzie's not planning to move in with her owner.

Chaplain Jacob Cohen has seen it all

Jacob Cohen is a chaplain with a bachelor's degree in psychology, a master-of-divinity degree and a passing resemblance to actor Robert DeNiro. On Sept. 11, 2001, he found himself seven miles from the World Trade Center towers the day they were destroyed, 3,000 lives were lost and countless others were changed forever. He managed to get to the site and minister to workers and survivors for nearly a month — even though he'd neglected to bring his chaplaincy ID along with him on what was supposed to be a vacation with his wife.

Cohen was born in Israel nearly 56 years ago. His family moved to the United States when he was a boy. "I still treasure the immigrant experience of seeing the Statue of Liberty" as the ship approached the Brooklyn Pier, he says.

He says he learned a lot about people and religion in the years he drove a cab to pay his way through college. "My job as a chaplain is to counsel law-enforcement officers, not inmates," he tells me early this week, over lunch at Chevys in Gold River. "If your cousin gets thrown in jail, I'm not the one to call. But I can certainly put you in touch with someone who'll help."

Like a lot of people whose work is deadly serious, Cohen smiles and jokes easily. He works with the nonprofit Sierra Law Enforcement Chaplaincy, counseling law officers at crime scenes and afterward, to minimize post-traumatic stress. The organization is supported by donations and its chaplains are on-call to myriad law enforcement agencies. Cohen is also a part-time hospice chaplain. He says that 9/11 made an indelible imprint on his memory and his dedication to his profession.

Cohen and Stephanie — his wife of 27 years, who works in the fashion industry — had arrived in New York City the morning of Sept. 11 on one of their regular homecoming vacations. They were relaxing at Stephanie's parents' place, on the border of Yonkers and the Bronx, seven miles from what came to be called Ground Zero, when Cohen says he heard a plane fly over, "very loud and very low. I actually thought it might be a commercial flight making an emergency landing at La Guardia Airport. I said a quick prayer that if the plane was in trouble it wasn't a commercial jet crammed with people." He was stretching out on a sofa when Stephanie ran into the room and told him to turn on the television. "The first tower had been hit."

Because Cohen is from Israel, where an understanding of terrorism is the unsentimental portion of one's daily education, he suspected that the next thing to happen would be bombs going off. "Then the second plane hit, and I have to admit, I said a few things a chaplain shouldn't say."

Tomorrow: Keeping the faith in a world of smoke and tragedy.

Aug. 9, 2012

Jacob Cohen, a chaplain for law enforcement agencies in Placer, Sacramento and El Dorado counties, made his way to the site of the fallen World Trade Center towers the day after 9/11/01. He volunteered his services. When he told a police officer, "I usually minister to survivors," the cop just stood there and didn't say anything. I realized he was telling me, in that look, that anyone who got out of the towers in time survived, and those who didn't weren't likely to have.

"I didn't know where to go to help," he continues. As I noted in yesterday's post, he had left his chaplaincy ID back in California — in the coming days, the El Dorado County Sheriff's office faxed it to authorities in New York City. "So I went to different police precincts and fire stations. The people I talked to had the 1,000-yard stare on their faces, meaning they couldn't focus on anything. Every fire station, and I mean every single one I visited, had lost seven or 10 or more of their team. But there they were, their brothers and sisters, continuing to gear up and head back in. It was remarkable."

He put his wife on a plane back to the Sacramento area. "We had come to New York this time to take a cruise to Aruba," he says. "Somehow, that didn't seem to matter. But I've told Steph for the past 11 years that I still owe her a cruise." He stayed in the city until Oct. 8, and then took Amtrak back to California. "What I left behind and what I came back to were completely different worlds," he says. "At one point I watched with curiosity as a crane operator did some work on the roof of the train station. And I couldn't figure out why it seemed so odd to me.

"Then I got it. For the past month, I hadn't seen a crane operating on a normal construction project."

If you're interested in hearing more about Cohen's work and experiences, you can reach him through the Sierra Law Enforcement Chaplaincy at (530) 621-1036.

Richard Rosebush:
A special kind of car salesman

Richard Rosebush is like no other car dealer I've ever met. Maybe that's because the vehicles he sells serve a humanitarian purpose: they're specially equipped vans and buses for physically disabled drivers.

Rosebush, 61, has been in the automotive industry for a quarter century. For the past year he's been the general manager of Destinations Mobility, an arm of Paratransit Inc., the nonprofit that's been shuttling the disabled and elderly around the Sacramento region since 1978. (For more information, check out the website destinationsmobility. com.)

"I realize that when you talk about nonprofits and car dealers, it's usually not in the same sentence," he tells me with a slight smile the other day as we sit in his office on Florin Road, right next door to Paratransit's headquarters. Since starting his new job, he's already sold about 45 specially equipped vehicles, to agencies such as Regional Transit, and individuals who can keep driving if their vehicles are modified to accommodate their particular physical challenge. "Everything we sell is wheelchair accessible," Rosebush says.

Because Destinations Mobility is, like its parent company, a nonprofit, its revenues are poured back into Paratransit so that it can continue to fulfill its mission. "The goal is to have enough money coming in so that Paratransit can offer free services to more disabled people who can't afford them," he says. He'd also like to take the Destinations/ Paratransit business model to southern California and, eventually, "across the country." I ask if he means as a franchise. "Well, kind of. We'd be consultants," he says.

Early on, Rosebush says he received permission from Paratransit's board of directors to sell the vehicles in his lot for less than a private dealership would demand. "Some of the special vehicles out there retail for as much as $50,000 to $80,000," he says. "That's an industry average. But I have about eight of them that I'll sell for $15,000 or less."

Rosebush is engaged to Anne Leeson, whom he met and worked with in Bay City, Michigan, where he was born and raised "She volunteers her time here," he says with undisguised affection. He owned an auto parts store back home "with five (service) bays," he proudly mentions. At one point he was the purchasing manager for five car dealerships. But what surprises me is that this soft-spoken, seemingly laid-back fellow is seriously into stock cars. In fact, he and his two brothers held a drag-racing record with the NHRA for seven years.

That stands for National Hot Rod Association. "My favorite car to drive was the '65 Chevelle," Rosebush recalls quietly, though I can certainly sense the wheels turning.

Dec. 26, 2012

Remembering Don Alden

From what I've learned in the past couple of years, Don Alden, who died in 2010, may have been one of the most interesting men I never met.

Alden was an engineer by trade and, well into his 80s, a competitive rower by temperament. At the Lake Natoma Aquatic Center, a couple of sculls and a scholarship are named after him. In the 1990s, Alden suggested the return from Siskiyou County of a truss bridge that had once spanned a portion of the American River in Folsom. It's back — and now called the Donald W. Alden Memorial Bridge.

One recent chilly afternoon, Alden's widow, Dorothy took me on a tour of the Lake Natomas facility where her husband had rowed long after most men his age either sank into a recliner, checked into a retirement home or simply checked out. In his own retirement — after 37 years with Caltrans, where he was a bridge designer and spec writer — Alden mentored young rowers and was a community activist who worked to protect Lake Natoma from the introduction of powerboats. If that sounds like a not-all-that-important accomplishment, let me ask you about the last time you enjoyed a quiet summer's morning at Donner Lake. Maybe this sounds familiar: WHEEEEENG-deeng-deeng-deeng-deeng-deeng, WHEEEEENG-deeng-deeng-deeng-deeng-deeng!

I've been friends for the past few years with Dorothy, whose name may ring a bell if you ever attended Sacramento Community Concerts, which she served as executive director for many years. While she was more than 10 years her husband's junior, if I tell you that Don was in his late 80s when he died, you'll deduce that his wife is a certified senior citizen. She's also a lively and not-frequent-enough lunch companion, as well as a nonjudgmental confidante of mine: not really old enough to be my mom but definitely in big sister territory.

While she's as adjusted as anyone can be who loses her spouse, travel companion and kindred spirit after more than 59 years of marriage, Dorothy still finds it difficult but uplifting to revisit the aquatic center. In the course of his rowing career, Don Alden won enough international medals to open his own trophy shop, and the memory of his accomplishments, good cheer and essential seriousness of purpose are reflected everywhere, particularly in the voices and faces of the young professionals and amateurs who staff and volunteer at the center.

In 1925, when Don was just four years old, F. Scott Fitzgerald ended "The Great Gatsby" with this line: "So we beat on, boats against the current, borne back ceaselessly into the past." I quote this because I think Don Alden might have liked it — and because I think you owe it to yourself to visit Lake Natoma Aquatic Center and the Folsom Truss Bridge, to see what this man did for his sport, his profession and his community.

Donna Yee is hungry for challenges

Donna Yee's 88-year-old mom, a widow, lives next door to her daughter's workplace. Yee is the chief executive officer of the Asian Community Center, which dedicates itself to the wellbeing of senior citizens (of all cultures, despite the implication of its name). Her mom lives in the center's 166-unit senior apartment community, ACC Greenhaven Terrace.

As if the New York City-born/San Francisco-raised Yee didn't have enough on her plate — this is her 14th year at the helm of the center — she agreed, a few years ago, to take over Meals On Wheels, a former Sacramento County program.

"The county called us and said, 'We're thinking of giving up Meals On Wheels and wonder if you'd be interested in taking it on.' I said, 'You've got to be kidding!' But they talked to other nonprofits about running it and we seemed to be the logical choice. Our missions were compatible."

ACC does all of the accounting, payroll and fund development for Meals On Wheels — or, as Yee puts it, "We're its mother ship." While each organization has professional staffs — ACC has 180 employees, and Meals On Wheels has 22 — each also relies on approximately 500 volunteers to fulfill its mission.

To qualify for a hot, five-times-a-week meal, all a person needs to be is 60 years old. "Age is the only requirement," yes says. "Participants aren't means-tested" — though lower-income seniors are its principal customers. A donation of $2.50 per meal "is suggested, not requested," she says.

Yee says that as successful as Meals On Wheels appears to be, "We're serving only about 2 percent of all the people in

Sacramento County who are 60 or older and could be using our program."

A lively, good-humored woman, with a thatch of thick, short hair and a wide, ingratiating smile, Yee earned a Ph.D. in social policy from Brandeis University's highly regarded Heller School. She's been in the long-term care business for 40 years. In tomorrow's column, we'll learn a bit more about her lifelong commitment to seniors — and why she thinks, from the standpoint of medical health, seniors today "stand on the shoulders of our parents."

Feb. 28, 2013

"We're excellent examples of all the medical advances that have been made since the 1920s," Donna Yee is telling me in the joint conference room of the Asian Community Center, of which she's CEO, and Meals On Wheels, which she also runs. "We stand on our parents' shoulders. In their lifetimes, the possibility of treating once-fatal diseases as chronic conditions and of managing disabilities really came of age."

But, she adds, "We're still in a period where some people, many people, don't have access to good medical care. We have this whole range of adults who are up and around — only 5 percent of the older population are in nursing homes — but we also have seniors who are sometimes younger but far less healthy because they lived in poverty or near-poverty all their lives."

She gets quiet for a moment — then says, with a sad smile that indicates she knows it's obvious but also true, "There is a significant bifurcation in our country between haves and have-nots."

Meals On Wheels serves 1,900 meals a day throughout Sacramento County. In yesterday's column Yee mentioned that the program is serving "only about 2 percent of all the people in Sacramento County who are 60 or older and could be using our program." She later pointed out that 2 percent is all that Meals On Wheels has the capacity, with current funding, to serve. She says she'd like to find an organization or individual to establish an endowment for the Meals On Wheels program so that it can expand.

Yee says that last year, the Area 4 Agency on Aging estimated that there were nearly 230,000 people of 60 years or more in Sacramento County — of whom 6 percent, or about 14,000, that are at or below the poverty line.

Yee's grandparents were immigrants from a village in China. Born in New York City, she grew up — and discovered her calling, she says — in San Francisco. "My parents each had two jobs so I was on my own quite a bit," she says. "I did a lot of 'hanging' in Chinatown, where I saw firsthand the conditions that many older people endured."

If donors and angels step forward, it could be that the next generations of senior citizens will be standing on Yee's slender but determined shoulders. You can get more information by visiting the Meals On Wheels website at mowsac.org or by phoning 916-444-9533.

Meet jeweler Nick Guzzetta

Jeweler Nick Guzzetta likes to tell people he's the illegitimate son of the late crooner Dean Martin. He named his 40-ft. Sea Ray pleasure boat, "That's Amore," in homage to one of Martin's most popular records. And when Joe Chiodo, co-publisher of Sacramento Magazine, got married a year-and-a-half ago, Guzzetta sang "Everybody Loves Somebody" (another Martin hit) to Chiodo's mom.

Full disclosure: It was a duet.

Fuller disclosure: I was one half of it. And yes, wine does improve one's voice — as long as everyone listening to it has had plenty of it.

Guzzetta started his eponymous jewelry store in 1988. He now has two: one on Howe Avenue in Sacramento and one on Douglas Boulevard in Roseville. A compactly built man with a smile so constant that his eyes seem in permanent squint mode, he makes friends with everyone he meets, sometimes with disarming dispatch.

Like the time he and his son Gary — "My best friend in the world," who manages the Roseville store — were in Monterey and decided to go to dinner at the famed Sardine Factory but lacked a reservation. They started chatting and laughing it up with people at the bar and pretty soon the owner, Bert Cutino, came over to see what all the fun was about, introduced himself, set up a table for father and son in a space where there'd been none and, at evening's end, personally drove them back to their hotel, everyone agreeing to get together again soon.

"One of the things I enjoy most is going out and meeting people," he says, perhaps needlessly.

Community leaders and members

Guzzetta is the grandson of Italian immigrants. "My grandma, who was from Palermo, told me when I was a little boy, 'All you have to do is treat people like you'd want them to treat you. Do that and you'll go far in life.' " It's a sweet remembrance, made more so by Guzzetta telling it without the slightest hint of irony (after all, it's simply a rephrasing of the Golden Rule). Part of his charm is that despite being a clever businessman and an amiable companion, he comes across as completely guileless.

I ask Guzzetta what's changed in the jewelry business since he first got into it in 1968 (he worked for Kay Jewelers and then spent 16 years with Zales; by the time he left, he was a regional vice president, with the entire state of California as his territory). "It's the way we market," he says. "In the old days, you could take out an ad in the newspaper, do a magazine ad and maybe a little radio — and you'd saturated the market. Not anymore."

Tomorrow: Nick goes viral.

March 5, 2013

You know what really rankles (a word I've been dying to use for years)? It's that if Nick Guzzetta is reading this two-part column about himself, he's doing it on the beach at Maui, with his wife, son and daughter-in-law nearby. He left a few days after we chatted over lunch at the newly remodeled Piatti Ristorante in Pavilions Shopping Mall.

Guzzetta, owner of self-named jewelry stores in Sacramento and Roseville, and his wife of 43 years, Jill, are the kind of people who really know how to live. They built a home in Greenhaven and remodeled it "a few times" over the ensuing decades. A native Sacramentan, Guzzetta had resisted an offer early in his career (at Zales Jewelers) to

279

relocate to its corporate headquarters in Dallas. "I told them that since my sales territory was California, it made no sense for me, business-wise, to live somewhere else. The truth is, I just didn't want to leave my family and friends."

If that's an old-fashioned sentiment, don't let it fool you into thinking that Guzzetta — except for a genuine commitment to customer service — takes an old-school approach to commerce. He's been on Facebook "for a couple of years" and is more conversant with social media than most 65-year-olds. "Well, it works," he says, breaking into one of his frequent laughs.

"You don't see that many young people reading newspapers these days, even on their various devices," he says. "Sometime back, I asked some of my younger employees what radio stations they listened to. "They said, 'We don't. We program what we want to hear and play it when we want to hear it.' That was one of the many times I realized the world had changed."

Guzzetta is known as being a reliable contributor to local charities, something he continued to do even when the recession broke the back of retail. "The so-called upper-class buyer was our savior," he says. "We kept wondering, 'Where did the middle class go?' We tried a lower price point and that helped for some of our items. And when it came right down to it, people would always come back to buy that anniversary gift, that birthday gift, that Valentine's Day gift. They just wouldn't spend as much."

Between the two stores, Guzzetta has nine full-time and two part-time employees. His son Gary, as we learned yesterday, runs the Roseville store. His daughter, Kelli Thompson, works beside her dad in the Sacramento operation.

"I think the key to our success is that we're run by a family," he says. "We're all in it together." Yes, and at least

Community leaders and members

four of them are in Maui right this minute. Have I said it
rankles?

23950687R00170

Made in the USA
San Bernardino, CA
05 September 2015